THE NATIONAL STRATEGY TO

SECURE CYBERSPACE

FEBRUARY 2003

THE WHITE HOUSE
WASHINGTON

My Fellow Americans:

The way business is transacted, government operates, and national defense is conducted have changed. These activities now rely on an interdependent network of information technology infrastructures called cyberspace. The *National Strategy to Secure Cyberspace* provides a framework for protecting this infrastructure that is essential to our economy, security, and way of life.

In the past few years, threats in cyberspace have risen dramatically. The policy of the United States is to protect against the debilitating disruption of the operation of information systems for critical infrastructures and, thereby, help to protect the people, economy, and national security of the United States. We must act to reduce our vulnerabilities to these threats before they can be exploited to damage the cyber systems supporting our Nation's critical infrastructures and ensure that such disruptions of cyberspace are infrequent, of minimal duration, manageable, and cause the least damage possible.

Securing cyberspace is an extraordinarily difficult strategic challenge that requires a coordinated and focused effort from our entire society—the federal government, state and local governments, the private sector, and the American people. To engage Americans in securing cyberspace, a draft version of this strategy was released for public comment, and ten town hall meetings were held around the Nation to gather input on the development of a national strategy. Thousands of people and numerous organizations participated in these town hall meetings and responded with comments. I thank them all for their continuing participation.

The cornerstone of America's cyberspace security strategy is and will remain a public-private partnership. The federal government invites the creation of, and participation in, public-private partnerships to implement this strategy. Only by acting together can we build a more secure future in cyberspace.

Table of Contents

Executive Summary

Our Nation's critical infrastructures are composed of public and private institutions in the sectors of agriculture, food, water, public health, emergency services, government, defense industrial base, information and telecommunications, energy, transportation, banking and finance, chemicals and hazardous materials, and postal and shipping. Cyberspace is their nervous system—the control system of our country. Cyberspace is composed of hundreds of thousands of interconnected computers, servers, routers, switches, and fiber optic cables that allow our critical infrastructures to work. Thus, the healthy functioning of cyberspace is essential to our economy and our national security.

This *National Strategy to Secure Cyberspace* is part of our overall effort to protect the Nation. It is an implementing component of the *National Strategy for Homeland Security* and is complemented by a *National Strategy for the Physical Protection of Critical Infrastructures and Key Assets.* The purpose of this document is to engage and empower Americans to secure the portions of cyberspace that they own, operate, control, or with which they interact. Securing cyberspace is a difficult strategic challenge that requires coordinated and focused effort from our entire society—the federal government, state and local governments, the private sector, and the American people.

The *National Strategy to Secure Cyberspace* outlines an initial framework for both organizing and prioritizing efforts. It provides direction to the federal government departments and agencies that have roles in cyberspace security. It also identifies steps that state and local governments, private companies and organizations, and individual Americans can take to improve our collective cybersecurity. The *Strategy* highlights the role of public-private engagement. The document provides a framework for the contributions that we all can make to secure our parts of cyberspace. The dynamics of cyberspace will require adjustments and amendments to the *Strategy* over time.

The speed and anonymity of cyber attacks makes distinguishing among the actions of terrorists, criminals, and nation states difficult, a task which often occurs only after the fact, if at all. Therefore, the *National Strategy to Secure Cyberspace* helps reduce our Nation's vulnerability to debilitating attacks against our critical information infrastructures or the physical assets that support them.

Strategic Objectives

Consistent with the *National Strategy for Homeland Security*, the strategic objectives of this *National Strategy to Secure Cyberspace* are to:

- Prevent cyber attacks against America's critical infrastructures;

- Reduce national vulnerability to cyber attacks; and

- Minimize damage and recovery time from cyber attacks that do occur.

Threat and Vulnerability

Our economy and national security are fully dependent upon information technology and the information infrastructure. At the core of the information infrastructure upon which we depend is the Internet, a system originally designed to share unclassified research among scientists who were assumed to be uninterested in abusing the network. It is that same Internet that today connects millions of other computer networks making most of the nation's essential services and infrastructures work. These computer networks also control physical objects such as electrical transformers, trains, pipeline pumps, chemical vats, radars, and stock markets, all of which exist beyond cyberspace.

A spectrum of malicious actors can and do conduct attacks against our critical information infrastructures. Of primary concern is the threat of organized cyber attacks capable of causing debilitating disruption to our Nation's critical infrastructures, economy, or national security. The required technical sophistication to carry out such an attack is high—and partially explains the lack of a debilitating attack to date. We should not, however, be too sanguine. There have been instances where organized attackers have exploited vulnerabilities that may be indicative of more destructive capabilities.

Uncertainties exist as to the intent and full technical capabilities of several observed attacks. Enhanced cyber threat analysis is needed to address long-term trends related to threats and vulnerabilities. What is known is that the attack tools and methodologies are becoming widely available, and the technical capability and sophistication of users bent on causing havoc or disruption is improving.

In peacetime America's enemies may conduct espionage on our Government, university research centers, and private companies. They may also seek to prepare for cyber strikes during a confrontation by mapping U.S. information systems, identifying key targets, and lacing our infrastructure with back doors and other means of access. In wartime or crisis, adversaries may seek to intimidate the Nation's political leaders by attacking critical infrastructures and key economic functions or eroding public confidence in information systems.

Cyber attacks on United States information networks can have serious consequences such as disrupting critical operations, causing loss of revenue and intellectual property, or loss of life. Countering such attacks requires the development of robust capabilities where they do not exist today if we are to reduce vulnerabilities and deter those with the capabilities and intent to harm our critical infrastructures.

The Government Role in Securing Cyberspace

In general, the private sector is best equipped and structured to respond to an evolving cyber threat. There are specific instances, however, where federal government response is most appropriate and justified. Looking inward, providing continuity of government requires ensuring the safety of its own cyber infrastructure and those assets required for supporting its essential missions and services. Externally, a government role in cybersecurity is warranted in cases where high transaction costs or legal barriers lead to significant coordination problems; cases in which governments operate in the absence of private sector forces; resolution of incentive problems that lead to under provisioning of critical shared resources; and raising awareness.

Public-private engagement is a key component of our Strategy to secure cyberspace. This is true for several reasons. Public-private partnerships can usefully confront coordination problems. They can significantly enhance information exchange and cooperation. Public-private engagement will take a variety of forms and will address awareness, training, technological improvements, vulnerability remediation, and recovery operations.

A federal role in these and other cases is only justified when the benefits of intervention outweigh the associated costs. This standard is especially important in cases where there are viable private sector solutions for addressing any potential threat or vulnerability. For each case,

consideration should be given to the broad-based costs and impacts of a given government action, versus other alternative actions, versus non-action, taking into account any existing or future private solutions.

Federal actions to secure cyberspace are warranted for purposes including: forensics and attack attribution, protection of networks and systems critical to national security, indications and warnings, and protection against organized attacks capable of inflicting debilitating damage to the economy. Federal activities should also support research and technology development that will enable the private sector to better secure privately-owned portions of the Nation's critical infrastructure.

Department of Homeland Security and Cyberspace Security

On November 25, 2002, President Bush signed legislation creating the Department of Homeland Security (DHS). This new cabinet-level department will unite 22 federal entities for the common purpose of improving our homeland security. The Secretary of DHS will have important responsibilities in cyberspace security. These responsibilities include:

- Developing a comprehensive national plan for securing the key resources and critical infrastructure of the United States;

- Providing crisis management in response to attacks on critical information systems;

- Providing technical assistance to the private sector and other government entities with respect to emergency recovery plans for failures of critical information systems;

- Coordinating with other agencies of the federal government to provide specific warning information and advice about appropriate protective measures and countermeasures to state, local, and nongovernmental organizations including the private sector, academia, and the public; and

- Performing and funding research and development along with other agencies that will lead to new scientific understanding and technologies in support of homeland security.

Consistent with these responsibilities, DHS will become a federal center of excellence for cybersecurity and provide a focal point for federal outreach to state, local, and nongovernmental organizations including the private sector, academia, and the public.

Critical Priorities for Cyberspace Security

The *National Strategy to Secure Cyberspace* articulates five national priorities including:

I. A National Cyberspace Security Response System;

II. A National Cyberspace Security Threat and Vulnerability Reduction Program;

III. A National Cyberspace Security Awareness and Training Program;

IV. Securing Governments' Cyberspace; and

V. National Security and International Cyberspace Security Cooperation.

The first priority focuses on improving our response to cyber incidents and reducing the potential damage from such events. The second, third, and fourth priorities aim to reduce threats from, and our vulnerabilities to, cyber attacks. The fifth priority is to prevent cyber attacks that could impact national security assets and to improve the international management of and response to such attacks.

Priority I: A National Cyberspace Security Response System

Rapid identification, information exchange, and remediation can often mitigate the damage caused by malicious cyberspace activity. For those activities to be effective at a national level, the United States needs a partnership between government and industry to perform analyses, issue warnings, and coordinate response efforts. Privacy and civil liberties must be protected in the process. Because no cybersecurity plan can be impervious to concerted and intelligent attack, information systems must be able to operate while under attack and have the resilience to restore full operations quickly.

The *National Strategy to Secure Cyberspace* identifies eight major actions and initiatives for cyberspace security response:

1. Establish a public-private architecture for responding to national-level cyber incidents;

2. Provide for the development of tactical and strategic analysis of cyber attacks and vulnerability assessments;

3. Encourage the development of a private sector capability to share a synoptic view of the health of cyberspace;

4. Expand the Cyber Warning and Information Network to support the role of DHS in coordinating crisis management for cyberspace security;

5. Improve national incident management;

6. Coordinate processes for voluntary participation in the development of national public-private continuity and contingency plans;

7. Exercise cybersecurity continuity plans for federal systems; and

8. Improve and enhance public-private information sharing involving cyber attacks, threats, and vulnerabilities.

1. Enhance law enforcement's capabilities for preventing and prosecuting cyberspace attacks;

2. Create a process for national vulnerability assessments to better understand the potential consequences of threats and vulnerabilities;

3. Secure the mechanisms of the Internet by improving protocols and routing;

4. Foster the use of trusted digital control systems/supervisory control and data acquisition systems;

5. Reduce and remediate software vulnerabilities;

6. Understand infrastructure interdependencies and improve the physical security of cyber systems and telecommunications;

7. Prioritize federal cybersecurity research and development agendas; and

8. Assess and secure emerging systems.

Priority II: A National Cyberspace Security Threat and Vulnerability Reduction Program

By exploiting vulnerabilities in our cyber systems, an organized attack may endanger the security of our Nation's critical infrastructures. The vulnerabilities that most threaten cyberspace occur in the information assets of critical infrastructure enterprises themselves and their external supporting structures, such as the mechanisms of the Internet. Lesser-secured sites on the interconnected network of networks also present potentially significant exposures to cyber attacks. Vulnerabilities result from weaknesses in technology and because of improper implementation and oversight of technological products.

The *National Strategy to Secure Cyberspace* identifies eight major actions and initiatives to reduce threats and related vulnerabilities:

Priority III: A National Cyberspace Security Awareness and Training Program

Many cyber vulnerabilities exist because of a lack of cybersecurity awareness on the part of computer users, systems administrators, technology developers, procurement officials, auditors, chief information officers (CIOs), chief executive officers, and corporate boards. Such awareness-based vulnerabilities present serious risks to critical infrastructures regardless of whether they exist within the infrastructure itself. A lack of trained personnel and the absence of widely accepted, multi-level certification programs for cybersecurity professionals complicate the task of addressing cyber vulnerabilities.

The *National Strategy to Secure Cyberspace* identifies four major actions and initiatives for awareness, education, and training:

1. Promote a comprehensive national awareness program to empower all Americans—businesses, the general workforce, and the general population—to secure their own parts of cyberspace;

2. Foster adequate training and education programs to support the Nation's cybersecurity needs;

3. Increase the efficiency of existing federal cybersecurity training programs; and

4. Promote private-sector support for well-coordinated, widely recognized professional cybersecurity certifications.

Priority IV: Securing Governments' Cyberspace

Although governments administer only a minority of the Nation's critical infrastructure computer systems, governments at all levels perform essential services in the agriculture, food, water, public health, emergency services, defense, social welfare, information and telecommunications, energy, transportation, banking and finance, chemicals, and postal and shipping sectors that depend upon cyberspace for their delivery. Governments can lead by example in cyberspace security, including fostering a marketplace for more secure technologies through their procurement.

The *National Strategy to Secure Cyberspace* identifies five major actions and initiatives for the securing of governments' cyberspace:

1. Continuously assess threats and vulnerabilities to federal cyber systems;

2. Authenticate and maintain authorized users of federal cyber systems;

3. Secure federal wireless local area networks;

4. Improve security in government outsourcing and procurement; and

5. Encourage state and local governments to consider establishing information technology security programs and participate in information sharing and analysis centers with similar governments.

Priority V: National Security and International Cyberspace Security Cooperation

America's cyberspace links the United States to the rest of the world. A network of networks spans the planet, allowing malicious actors on one continent to act on systems thousands of miles away. Cyber attacks cross borders at light speed, and discerning the source of malicious activity is difficult. America must be capable of safeguarding and defending its critical systems and networks. Enabling our ability to do so requires a system of international cooperation to facilitate information sharing, reduce vulnerabilities, and deter malicious actors.

The *National Strategy to Secure Cyberspace* identifies six major actions and initiatives to strengthen U.S. national security and international cooperation:

1. Strengthen cyber-related counterintelligence efforts;

2. Improve capabilities for attack attribution and response;

3. Improve coordination for responding to cyber attacks within the U.S. national security community;

4. Work with industry and through international organizations to facilitate dialogue and partnerships among international public and private sectors focused on protecting information infrastructures and promoting a global "culture of security;"

5. Foster the establishment of national and international watch-and-warning networks to detect and prevent cyber attacks as they emerge; and

6. Encourage other nations to accede to the Council of Europe Convention on Cybercrime, or to ensure that their laws and procedures are at least as comprehensive.

A National Effort

Protecting the widely distributed assets of cyberspace requires the efforts of many Americans. The federal government alone cannot sufficiently defend America's cyberspace. Our traditions of federalism and limited government require that organizations outside the federal government take the lead in many of these efforts. Every American who can contribute to securing part of cyberspace is encouraged to do so. The federal government invites the creation of, and participation in, public-private partnerships to raise cyberse-curity awareness, train personnel, stimulate market forces, improve technology, identify and remediate vulnerabilities, exchange information, and plan recovery operations.

People and organizations across the United States have already taken steps to improve cyberspace security. On September 18, 2002, many private-sector entities released plans and strategies for securing their respective infra-structures. The Partnership for Critical Infrastructure Security has played a unique role in facilitating private-sector contributions to

this Strategy. Inputs from the critical sector's themselves can be found at http://www.pcis.org. (These documents were not subject to government approval.)

These comprehensive infrastructure plans describe the strategic initiatives of various sectors, including:

- Banking and Finance;

- Insurance;

- Chemical;

- Oil and Gas;

- Electric;

- Law Enforcement;

- Higher Education;

- Transportation (Rail);

- Information Technology and Telecommunications; and

- Water.

As each of the critical infrastructure sectors implements these initiatives, threats and vulner-abilities to our infrastructures will be reduced.

For the foreseeable future two things will be true: America will rely upon cyberspace and the federal government will seek a continuing broad partnership with the private sector to develop, implement, and refine a *National Strategy to Secure Cyberspace*.

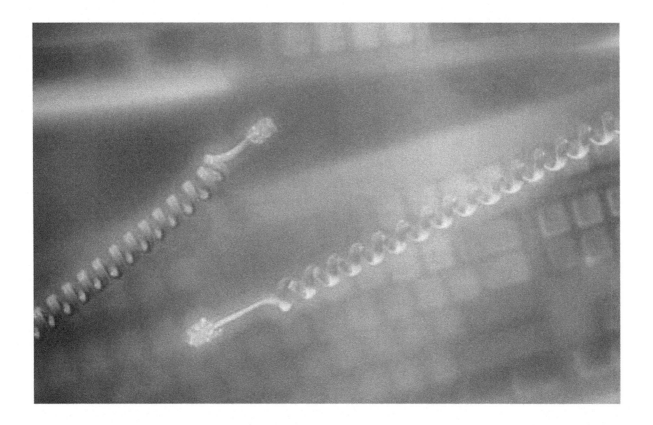

Introduction

A Nation in Cyberspace

Our Nation's critical infrastructures consist of the physical and cyber assets of public and private institutions in several sectors: agriculture, food, water, public health, emergency services, government, defense industrial base, information and telecommunications, energy, transportation, banking and finance, chemicals and hazardous materials, and postal and shipping. Cyberspace is the nervous system of these infrastructures—the control system of our country. Cyberspace comprises hundreds of thousands of interconnected computers, servers, routers, switches, and fiber optic cables that make our critical infrastructures work. Thus, the healthy functioning of cyberspace is essential to our economy and our national security. Unfortunately, recent events have highlighted the existence of cyberspace vulnerabilities and the fact that malicious actors seek to exploit them. (See, *Cyberspace Threats and Vulnerabilities.*)

This *National Strategy to Secure Cyberspace* is part of an overall effort to protect the Nation. It is an implementing component of the *National Strategy for Homeland Security* and is complemented by the *National Strategy for the Physical Protection of Critical Infrastructures and Key Assets.* The purpose of this document is to engage and empower Americans to secure the portions of cyberspace that they own, operate, or control, or with which they interact. Securing cyberspace is a difficult strategic challenge that requires coordinated and focused effort from our entire society—the federal government, state and local governments, the private sector, and the American people.

A Unique Problem, a Unique Process

Most critical infrastructures, and the cyberspace on which they rely, are privately owned and operated. The technologies that create and support cyberspace evolve rapidly from private-sector and academic innovation. Government alone cannot sufficiently secure cyberspace. Thus, President Bush has called for voluntary partnerships among government, industry, academia, and nongovernmental groups to secure and defend cyberspace. (See, *National Policy and Guiding Principles*.)

In recognition of this need for partnership, the process to develop the *National Strategy to Secure Cyberspace* included soliciting views from both the public and private sectors. To do so, the White House sponsored town hall meetings on cyberspace security in ten metropolitan areas. Consequently, individual sectors (e.g., higher education, state and local government, banking and finance) formed workgroups to create initial sector-specific cyberspace security strategies. Additionally, the White House created a Presidential advisory panel, the National Infrastructure Advisory Council, consisting of leaders from the key sectors of the economy, government, and academia. The President's National Security Telecommunications Advisory Committee reviewed and commented on the *Strategy*.

In September 2002, the President's Critical Infrastructure Protection Board sought comments from individuals and institutions nationwide by placing a draft version of the *Strategy* online for review. Thousands participated in the town hall meetings and provided comments online. Their comments contributed to shaping the *Strategy* by narrowing its focus and sharpening its priorities.

This process recognizes that we can only secure cyberspace successfully through an inclusive national effort that engages major institutions throughout the country. The federal government designed the *Strategy* development process to raise the Nation's level of awareness of the importance of cybersecurity. Its intent was to produce a *Strategy* that many Americans could feel they had a direct role in developing, and to which they would be committed.

Although the redrafting process reflects many of the comments provided, not everyone will agree with each component of the *National Strategy to Secure Cyberspace*. Many issues could not be addressed in detail, and others are not yet ripe for national policy. The *Strategy* is not immutable; actions will evolve as technologies advance, as threats and vulnerabilities change, and as our understanding of the cybersecurity issues improves and clarifies. A national dialogue on cyberspace security must therefore continue.

In the weeks following the release of the draft *Strategy*, Congress approved the creation of the Department of Homeland Security (DHS), assigned to it many agencies that are active in cybersecurity, and directed it to perform new cybersecurity missions. This *Strategy* reflects those changes. Congress passed and the President signed the *Cyber Security Research and Development Act* (Public Law 107-305), authorizing a multi-year effort to create more secure cyber technologies, to expand cybersecurity research and development, and to improve the cybersecurity workforce.

Five National Cyberspace Security Priorities

The *National Strategy to Secure Cyberspace* is a call for national awareness and action by individuals and institutions throughout the United States, to increase the level of cybersecurity nationwide and to implement continuous processes for identifying and remedying cyber vulnerabilities. Its framework is an agenda of five broad priorities that require widespread voluntary participation. Each individual program consists of several components, many of which were drawn from the draft *Strategy's* recommendations and related public comments.

Addressing these priorities requires the leadership of DHS as well as several other key federal departments and agencies. As part of the Office of Management and Budget (OMB)-led budget process, and with the support of Congress, these departments and agencies now have the task of translating the *Strategy's* recommendations into actions.

Corporations, universities, state and local governments, and other partners are also encouraged to take actions consistent with these five national cyberspace security priorities, both independently and in partnership with the federal government. Each private-sector organization must make its own decisions based on cost effectiveness analysis and risk-management and mitigation strategies.

The *National Strategy to Secure Cyberspace* articulates five national priorities. The first priority focuses on improving our ability to respond to cyber incidents and reduce the potential damage from such events. The second, third, and fourth priorities aim to reduce the numbers of cyber threats and our overall vulnerability to cyber attacks. The fifth priority focuses on preventing cyber attacks with the potential to impact national security assets and improving international management of and response to such attacks.

Priority I: A National Cyberspace Security Response System

Rapid identification, information exchange, and remediation can often mitigate the damage caused by malicious cyberspace activity. For those activities to take place effectively at a national level, the United States requires a partnership between government and industry to perform analyses, issue warnings, and coordinate response efforts. Privacy and civil liberties must be protected in the process. Because no cybersecurity plan can be impervious to concerted and intelligent attacks, information systems must be able to operate while under attack and also have the resilience to restore full operations in their wake. To prepare for the possibility of major cyber attacks, America needs a national cyber disaster recovery plan. The National Cyberspace Security Response System will involve public and private institutions and cyber centers to perform analysis, conduct watch and warning activities, enable information exchange, and facilitate restoration efforts.

Priority II: A National Cyberspace Security Threat and Vulnerability Reduction Program

By exploiting vulnerabilities in our cyber systems, an organized cyber attack may endanger the security of our Nation's critical infrastructures. Cyberspace vulnerabilities occur in the critical infrastructure enterprises and government departments themselves, in their external supporting structures (such as the mechanisms of the Internet), and in unsecured sites across the interconnected network of networks. Vulnerabilities exist for several reasons including technological weaknesses, poor security-control implementation, and absences of effective oversight.

A National Cyberspace Security Threat and Vulnerability reduction program will include coordinated national efforts conducted by governments and the private sector to identify and remediate the most serious cyber vulnerabilities through collaborative activities, such as sharing best practices and evaluating and implementing new technologies. Additional program components will include raising cybersecurity awareness, increasing criminal justice activities, and developing national security programs to deter future cyber threats.

Priority III: A National Cyberspace Security Awareness and Training Program

Many information-system vulnerabilities exist because of a lack of cyberspace security awareness on the part of computer users, systems administrators, technology developers, procurement officials, auditors, chief information officers, chief executive officers, and corporate boards. These vulnerabilities can present serious risks to the infrastructures even if they are not actually part of the infrastructure itself. A lack of trained personnel and the absence of widely accepted, multi-level certifications for personnel further complicate the task of reducing vulnerabilities.

The National Cyberspace Security Awareness and Training Program will raise cybersecurity awareness in companies, government agencies, universities, and among the Nation's computer users. It will further address shortfalls in the numbers of trained and certified cybersecurity personnel.

Priority IV: Securing Governments' Cyberspace

Although governments administer only a minority of the Nation's critical infrastructure computer systems, governments at all levels perform essential services that rely on each of the critical infrastructure sectors, which are agriculture, food, water, public health, emergency services, government, defense industrial base, information and telecommunications, energy, transportation, banking and finance, chemicals and hazardous materials, and postal and shipping. With respect to investment in cyberspace security, government can lead by

example by fostering a marketplace for more secure technologies through large procurements of advanced information assurance technologies. A program to implement such products will help to ensure that federal computer systems and networks are secure. The federal government will also assist state and local governments with cybersecurity awareness, training, and information exchange.

Priority V: National Security and International Cyberspace Security Cooperation

America's cyberspace links the United States to the rest of the world. A network of networks spans the planet, allowing malicious actors on one continent to act on systems thousands of miles away. Cyber attacks cross borders at light speed, and discerning the source of malicious activity is difficult. America must be capable of safeguarding and defending its critical systems and networks—regardless of where an attack originates. Facilitating our ability to do so requires a system of international cooperation to enable the information sharing, reduce vulnerabilities, and deter malicious actors.

Actions and Recommendations

The *Strategy* highlights actions that the federal government will take and makes recommendations to our partners in nongovernmental organizations. The actions and recommendations (A/R) are italicized throughout the Strategy and numbered according to the associated priority. For example A/R 1-1 is the first action or recommendation in Priority I. Appendix A provides a summary of all of the A/Rs proposed.

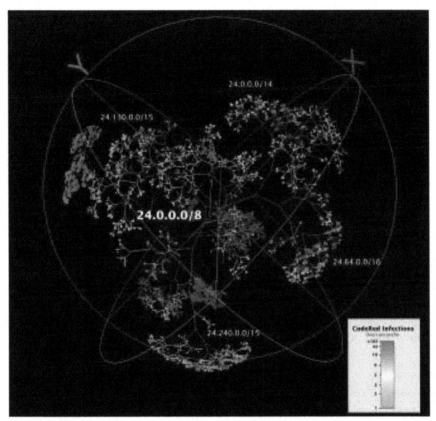

A Mapping of
Code Red
Penetration on a
Portion of the
Internet.

*Image courtesy
UCSD/CAIDA
(www.caida.org)
© 2002 The Regents
of the University of
California.*

Cyberspace Threats and Vulnerabilities

A Case for Action

The terrorist attacks against the United States that took place on September 11, 2001, had a profound impact on our Nation. The federal government and society as a whole have been forced to reexamine conceptions of security on our home soil, with many understanding only for the first time the lengths to which self-designated enemies of our country are willing to go to inflict debilitating damage.

We must move forward with the understanding that there are enemies who seek to inflict damage on our way of life. They are ready to attack us on our own soil, and they have shown a willingness to use unconventional means to execute those attacks. While the attacks of

September 11 were physical attacks, we are facing increasing threats from hostile adversaries in the realm of cyberspace as well.

A Nation Now Fully Dependent on Cyberspace

For the United States, the information technology revolution quietly changed the way business and government operate. Without a great deal of thought about security, the Nation shifted the control of essential processes in manufacturing, utilities, banking, and communications to networked computers. As a result, the cost of doing business dropped and productivity skyrocketed. The trend toward greater use of networked systems continues.

By 2003, our economy and national security became fully dependent upon information technology and the information infrastructure. A network of networks directly supports the operation of all sectors of our economy—energy (electric power, oil and gas), transportation (rail, air, merchant marine), finance and banking, information and telecommunications, public health, emergency services, water, chemical, defense industrial base, food, agriculture, and postal and shipping. The reach of these computer networks exceeds the bounds of cyberspace. They also control physical objects such as electrical transformers, trains, pipeline pumps, chemical vats, and radars.

Threats in Cyberspace

A spectrum of malicious actors can and do conduct attacks against our critical information infrastructures. Of primary concern is the threat of organized cyber attacks capable of causing debilitating disruption to our Nation's critical infrastructures, economy, or national security. The required technical sophistication to carry out such an attack is high—and partially explains the lack of a debilitating attack to date. We should not, however, be too sanguine. There have been instances where attackers have exploited vulnerabilities that may be indicative of more destructive capabilities.

Uncertainties exist as to the intent and full technical capabilities of several observed attacks. Enhanced cyber threat analysis is needed to address long-term trends related to threats and vulnerabilities. What is known is that the attack tools and methodologies are becoming widely available, and the technical capability and sophistication of users bent on causing havoc or disruption is improving.

As an example, consider the "NIMDA" ("ADMIN" spelled backwards) attack. Despite the fact that NIMDA did not create a catastrophic disruption to the critical infrastructure, it is a good example of the increased technical sophistication showing up in cyber attacks. It demonstrated that the arsenal of weapons available to organized attackers now contains the capability to learn and adapt to its local environment. NIMDA was an automated cyber attack, a blend of a computer worm and a computer virus. It propagated across the Nation with enormous speed and tried several different ways to infect computer systems it invaded until it gained access and destroyed files. It went from nonexistent to nationwide in an hour, lasted for days, and attacked 86,000 computers.

Speed is also increasing. Consider that two months before NIMDA, a cyber attack called Code Red infected 150,000 computer systems in 14 hours.

Because of the increasing sophistication of computer attack tools, an increasing number of actors are capable of launching nationally significant assaults against our infrastructures and cyberspace. In peacetime America's enemies may conduct espionage on our Government, university research centers, and private companies. They may also seek to prepare for cyber strikes during a confrontation by mapping U.S. information systems, identifying key targets, lacing our infrastructure with back doors and other means of access. In wartime or crisis, adversaries may seek to intimidate the nation's political leaders by attacking critical infrastructures and key economic functions or eroding public confidence in information systems.

Cyber attacks on U.S. information networks can have serious consequences such as disrupting critical operations, causing loss of revenue and intellectual property, or loss of life. Countering such attacks requires the development of robust capabilities where they do not exist today if we are to reduce vulnerabilities and deter those with the capabilities and intent to harm our critical infrastructures.

Cyberspace provides a means for organized attack on our infrastructure from a distance. These attacks require only commodity technology, and enable attackers to obfuscate their identities, locations, and paths of entry. Not only does cyberspace provide the ability to exploit weaknesses in our critical infrastructures, but it also provides a fulcrum for leveraging physical attacks by allowing the possibility of disrupting communications, hindering U.S. defensive or offensive response, or delaying emergency responders who would be essential following a physical attack.

In the last century, geographic isolation helped protect the United States from a direct physical invasion. In cyberspace national boundaries have little meaning. Information flows continuously and seamlessly across political, ethnic, and religious divides. Even the infrastructure that makes up cyberspace—software and hardware—is global in its design and development. Because of the global nature of cyberspace, the vulnerabilities that exist are open to the world and available to anyone, anywhere, with sufficient capability to exploit them.

Reduce Vulnerabilities in the Absence of Known Threats

While the Nation's critical infrastructures must, of course, deal with specific threats as they arise, waiting to learn of an imminent attack before addressing important critical infrastructure vulnerabilities is a risky and unacceptable strategy. Cyber attacks can burst onto the Nation's networks with little or no warning and spread so fast that many victims never have a chance to hear the alarms. Even with forewarning, they likely would not have had the time, knowledge, or tools needed to protect themselves. In some cases creating defenses against these attacks would have taken days.

A key lesson derived from these and other such cyber attacks is that organizations that rely on networked computer systems must take proactive steps to identify and remedy their vulnerabilities, rather than waiting for an attacker to be stopped or until alerted of an

impending attack. Vulnerability assessment and remediation activities must be ongoing. An information technology security audit conducted by trained professionals to identify infrastructure vulnerabilities can take months. Subsequently, the process of creating a multi-layered defense and a resilient network to remedy the most serious vulnerabilities could take several additional months. The process must then be regularly repeated.

Threat and Vulnerability: A Five-Level Problem

Managing threat and reducing vulnerability in cyberspace is a particularly complex challenge because of the number and range of different types of users. Cyberspace security requires action on multiple levels and by a diverse group of actors because literally hundreds of millions of devices are interconnected by a network of networks. The problem of cyberspace security can be best addressed on five levels.

Level 1, the Home User/Small Business

Though not a part of a critical infrastructure the computers of home users can become part of networks of remotely controlled machines that are then used to attack critical infrastructures. Undefended home and small business computers, particularly those using digital subscriber line (DSL) or cable connections, are vulnerable to attackers who can employ the use of those machines without the owner's knowledge. Groups of such "zombie" machines can then be used by third-party actors to launch denial-of-service (DoS) attacks on key Internet nodes and other important enterprises or critical infrastructures.

Level 2, Large Enterprises

Large-scale enterprises (corporations, government agencies, and universities) are common targets for cyber attacks. Many such enterprises are part of critical infrastructures. Enterprises require clearly articulated, active information security policies and programs to audit compliance with cybersecurity best practices. According to the U.S. intelligence community, American networks will be increasingly targeted by malicious actors both for the data and the power they possess.

Level 3, Critical Sectors/Infrastructures

When organizations in sectors of the economy, government, or academia unite to address common cybersecurity problems, they can often reduce the burden on individual enterprises. Such collaboration often produces shared institutions and mechanisms, which, in turn, could have cyber vulnerabilities whose exploitation could directly affect the operations of member enterprises and the sector as a whole. Enterprises can also reduce cyber risks by participating in groups that develop best practices, evaluate technological offerings, certify products and services, and share information.

Several sectors have formed Information Sharing and Analysis Centers (ISACs) to monitor for cyber attacks directed against their respective infrastructures. ISACs are also a vehicle for sharing information about attack trends, vulnerabilities, and best practices.

Level 4, National Issues and Vulnerabilities

Some cybersecurity problems have national implications and cannot be solved by individual enterprises or infrastructure sectors alone. All sectors share the Internet. Accordingly, they are all at risk if its mechanisms (e.g., protocols and routers) are not secure. Weaknesses in widely used software and hardware products can also create problems at the national level, requiring coordinated activities for the research and development of improved technologies. Additionally, the lack of trained and certified cybersecurity professionals also merits national-level concern.

Level 5, Global

The worldwide web is a planetary information grid of systems. Internationally shared standards enable interoperability among the world's computer systems. This interconnectedness, however, also means that problems on one continent have the potential to affect computers on another. We therefore rely on international cooperation to share information related to cyber issues and, further, to prosecute cyber criminals. Without such cooperation, our collective ability to detect, deter, and minimize the effects of cyber-based attacks would be greatly diminished.

New Vulnerabilities Requiring Continuous Response

New vulnerabilities are created or discovered regularly. The process of securing networks and systems, therefore, must also be continuous. The Computer Emergency Response Team/Coordination Center (CERT/CC) notes that not only are the numbers of cyber incidents and attacks increasing at an alarming rate, so too are the numbers of vulnerabilities that an attacker could exploit. Identified computer security vulnerabilities—faults in software and hardware that could permit unauthorized network access or allow an attacker to cause network damage—increased significantly from 2000 to 2002, with the number of vulnerabilities going from 1,090 to 4,129.

The mere installation of a network security device is not a substitute for maintaining and updating a network's defenses. Ninety percent of the participants in a recent Computer Security Institute survey reported using antivirus software on their network systems, yet 85 percent of their systems had been damaged by computer viruses. In the same survey, 89 percent of the respondents had installed computer firewalls, and 60 percent had intrusion detection systems. Nevertheless, 90 percent reported that security breaches had taken place, and 40 percent of their systems had

Roles and Responsibilites in Securing Cyberspace

	Priority 1 National Cyberspace Security Response System	Priority 2 National Cyberspace Security Threat and Vulnerability Reduction System	Priority 3 National Cyberspace Security Awareness and Training Program	Priority 4 Securing Governments' Cyberspace	Priority 5 National Security and International Cyberspace Security Cooperation
Home User/Small Business		X	X		
Large Enterprises	X	X	X	X	X
Critical Sectors/ Infrastructures	X	X	X	X	X
National Issues and Vulnerabilities	X	X	X	X	
Global					X

been penetrated from outside their network.

The majority of security vulnerabilities can be mitigated through good security practices. As these survey numbers indicate, however, practicing good security includes more than simply installing those devices. It also requires operating them correctly and keeping them current through regular patching and virus updates.

Cybersecurity and Opportunity Cost

For individual companies and the national economy as a whole, improving computer security requires investing attention, time, and money. For fiscal year 2003, President Bush requested that Congress increase funds to secure federal computers by 64 percent. President Bush's investment in securing federal computer networks now will eventually reduce overall expenditures through cost-saving E-Government solutions, modern enterprise management, and by reducing the number of opportunities for waste and fraud.

For the national economy—particularly its information technology industry component—the dearth of trusted, reliable, secure information systems presents a barrier to future growth. Much of the potential for economic growth made possible by the information technology revolution has yet to be realized—deterred in part by cyberspace security risks. Cyberspace vulnerabilities place more than transactions at risk; they jeopardize intellectual property, business operations, infrastructure services, and consumer trust.

Conversely, cybersecurity investments result in more than costly overhead expenditures. They produce a return on investment. Surveys repeatedly show that:

- Although the likelihood of suffering a severe cyber attack is difficult to estimate, the costs associated with a successful one are likely to be greater than the investment in a cybersecurity program to prevent it; and

• Designing strong security protocols into the information systems architecture of an enterprise can reduce its overall operational costs by enabling cost-saving processes, such as remote access and customer or supply-chain interactions, which could not occur in networks lacking appropriate security.

These results suggest that, with greater awareness of the issues, companies can benefit from increasing their levels of cybersecurity. Greater awareness and voluntary efforts are critical components of the *National Strategy to Secure Cyberspace*.

Individual and National Risk Management

Until recently overseas terrorist networks had caused limited damage in the United States. On September 11, 2001, that quickly changed. One estimate places the increase in cost to our economy from attacks to U.S. information systems at 400 percent over four years. While those losses remain relatively limited, that too could change abruptly.

Every day in the United States individual companies, and home computer users, suffer damage from cyber attacks that, to the victims, represent significant losses. Conditions likewise exist for relative measures of damage to occur on a national level, affecting the networks and systems on which the Nation depends:

• Potential adversaries have the intent;

• Tools that support malicious activities are broadly available; and,

• Vulnerabilities of the Nation's systems are many and well known.

No single strategy can completely eliminate cyberspace vulnerabilities and their associated threats. Nevertheless, the Nation must act to manage risk responsibly and to enhance its ability to minimize the damage that results

from attacks that do occur. Through this statement, we reveal nothing to potential foes that they and others do not already know. In 1997 a Presidential Commission identified the risks in a seminal public report. In 2000 the first national plan to address the problem was published. Citing these risks, President Bush issued an Executive Order in 2001, making cybersecurity a priority, and accordingly, increasing funds to secure federal networks. In 2002 the President moved to consolidate and strengthen federal cybersecurity agencies as part of the proposed Department of Homeland Security.

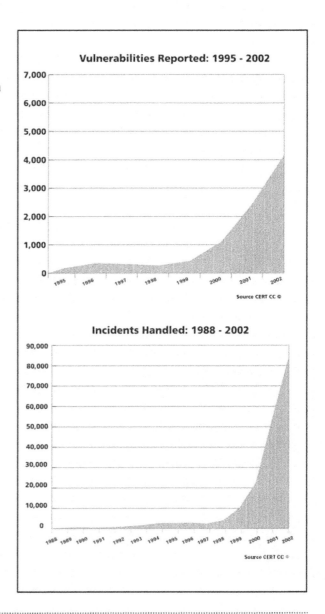

Government Alone Cannot Secure Cyberspace

Despite increased awareness around the importance of cybersecurity and the measures taken thus far to improve our capabilities, cyber risks continue to underlie our national information networks and the critical systems they manage. Reducing that risk requires an unprecedented, active partnership among diverse components of our country and our global partners.

The federal government could not—and, indeed, should not—secure the computer networks of privately owned banks, energy companies, transportation firms, and other parts of the private sector. The federal government should likewise not intrude into homes and small businesses, into universities, or state and local agencies and departments to create secure computer networks. Each American who depends on cyberspace, the network of information networks, must secure the part that they own or for which they are responsible.

National Policy and Guiding Principles

National Policy, Principles, and Organization

This section describes the national policy that shapes the *National Strategy to Secure Cyberspace* and the basic framework of principles within which it was developed. It also outlines the roles and missions of federal agencies.

National Policy

The information technology revolution has changed the way business is transacted, government operates, and national defense is conducted. These three functions now depend on an interdependent network of critical information infrastructures that we refer to as "cyberspace."

It is the policy of the United States to prevent or minimize disruptions to critical information infrastructures and thereby protect the people, the economy, the essential human and government services, and the national security of the United States. Disruptions that do occur should be infrequent, of minimal duration and manageable and cause the least damage possible. The policy requires a continuous effort to secure information systems for critical infrastructure and includes voluntary public-private partnerships involving corporate and nongovernmental organizations.

Consistent with the objectives of the *National Strategy for Homeland Security*, the objectives of the *National Strategy to Secure Cyberspace* are to:

- Prevent cyber attacks against our critical infrastructures;

- Reduce our national vulnerabilities to cyber attack; and,

- Minimize the damage and recovery time from cyber attacks that do occur.

Guiding Principles

In January 2001, the Administration began to review the role of information systems and cybersecurity. In October 2001, President Bush issued Executive Order 13231, authorizing a protection program that consists of continuous efforts to secure information systems for critical infrastructure, including emergency preparedness communications and the physical assets that support such systems. The Federal Information Security Management Act (FISMA) and Executive Order 13231, together with other relevant Presidential directives and statutory authorities, provide the framework for executive branch cyberspace security activities.

The protection of these cyber systems is essential to every sector of the economy. The development and implementation of this program directive has been guided by the following organizing principles:

1. *A National Effort:* Protecting the widely distributed assets of cyberspace requires the efforts of many Americans. The federal government alone cannot defend America's cyberspace. Our traditions of federalism and limited government require that organizations outside the federal government take the lead in many of these efforts. The government's role in securing cyberspace includes promoting better security in privately owned infra-structures when there is a need to:

   - Convene and facilitate discussions between and with nongovernmental entities;

   - Identify instances where the "tragedy of the commons" can affect homeland, national, and economic security; and

   - Share information about cyber threats and vulnerabilities so nongovernmental entities can adjust their risk management strategies and plans, as appropriate.

In every case, the scope for government involvement is limited to those cases when the benefits of intervention outweigh the direct and indirect costs.

Every American who can contribute to securing part of cyberspace is encouraged to do so. The federal government promotes the creation of, and participation in, public-private partnerships to raise awareness, train personnel, stimulate market forces, improve technology, identify and remediate vulnerabilities, exchange information, and plan recovery opera-tions. Many sectors have undertaken the important step of developing ISACs, which facilitate communication, the development of best practices, and the dissemination of security-related infor-mation. In addition, various sectors have developed plans to secure their parts of cyberspace, which complement this *Strategy*, and the government intends for this productive and collaborative partnership to continue.

2. *Protect Privacy and Civil Liberties:* The abuse of cyberspace infringes on our privacy and our liberty. It is incumbent on the federal government to avoid such abuse and infringement. Cybersecurity and personal privacy need not be opposing goals. Cyberspace security programs must strengthen, not weaken, such protections. Accordingly, care must be taken to respect privacy interests and

other civil liberties. Consumers and operators must have confidence their voluntarily shared, nonpublic information will be handled accurately, confidentially, and reliably. The federal government will lead by example in implementing strong privacy policies and practices in the agencies. As part of this process, the federal government will consult regularly with privacy advocates and experts.

3. *Regulation and Market Forces:* federal regulation will not become a primary means of securing cyberspace. Broad regulations mandating how all corporations must configure their information systems could divert more successful efforts by creating a lowest-common-denominator approach to cybersecurity, which evolving technology would quickly marginalize. Even worse, such an approach could result in less secure and more homogeneous security architectures than we have now. By law, some federal regulatory agencies already include cyber-security considerations in their oversight activity. However, the market itself is expected to provide the major impetus to improve cybersecurity.

4. *Accountability and Responsibility:* The *National Strategy to Secure Cyberspace* is focused on producing a more resilient and reliable information infrastructure. When possible, it designates lead executive branch departments or agencies for federal cyberspace security initiatives. On November 25, 2002, the President signed the *Homeland Security Act of 2002* establishing the Department of Homeland Security (DHS). DHS will be responsible for many of the initiatives outlined in the *National Strategy to Secure Cyberspace*. The *Strategy* also recommends actions federal, state and local governments, the private sector, and the American people can take to help secure cyberspace.

5. *Ensure Flexibility:* Cyber threats change rapidly. Accordingly, the *National Strategy to Secure Cyberspace* emphasizes flexibility in our ability to respond to cyber attacks and manage vulnerability reduction. The rapid development of attack tools provides potential attackers with a strategic advantage to adapt their offensive tactics quickly to target perceived weaknesses in networked information systems and organizations' abilities to respond. Flexible planning allows organizations to reassess priorities and realign resources as the cyber threat evolves.

6. *Multi-Year Planning:* Securing cyberspace is an ongoing process, as new technologies appear and new vulnerabilities are identified. The *National Strategy to Secure Cyberspace* provides an initial framework for achieving cyberspace security objectives. Departments and agencies should adopt multi-year cybersecurity plans for sustaining their respective roles. Other public- and private-sector organizations are also encouraged to consider multi-year plans.

Department of Homeland Security and Cyberspace Security

DHS unites 22 federal entities for the common purpose of improving homeland security. The Department also creates a focal point for managing cyberspace incidents that could impact the federal government or even the national information infrastructures. The Secretary of Homeland Security will have important responsibilities in cyberspace security, including:

• Developing a comprehensive national plan for securing the key resources and critical infrastructures of the United States, including information technology and telecommunications systems (including

CRITICAL INFRASTRUCTURE LEAD AGENCIES

LEAD AGENCY	SECTORS
Department of Homeland Security	• Information and Telecommunications • Transportation (aviation, rail, mass transit, waterborne commerce, pipelines, and highways (including trucking and intelligent transportation systems) • Postal and Shipping • Emergency Services • Continuity of Government
Department of the Treasury	• Banking and Finance
Department of Health and Human Services	• Public Health (including prevention, surveillance, laboratory services, and personal health services) • Food (all except for meat and poultry)
Department of Energy	• Energy (electric power, oil and gas production, and storage)
Environmental Protection Agency	• Water • Chemical Industry and Hazardous Materials
Department of Agriculture	• Agriculture • Food (meat and poultry)
Department of Defense	• Defense Industrial Base

satellites) and the physical and technological assets that support such systems;

• Providing crisis management support in response to threats to, or attacks on, critical information systems;

• Providing technical assistance to the private sector and other governmental entities with respect to emergency recovery plans that respond to major failures of critical information systems;

• Coordinating with other federal agencies to provide specific warning information and advice about appropriate protective measures and countermeasures to state and local government agencies and authorities, the private sector, other entities, and the public; and

• Performing and funding research and development along with other agencies that will lead to new scientific understanding and technologies in support of homeland security.

Designation of Coordinating Agencies

A productive partnership between the federal government and the private sector depends on effective coordination and communication. To facilitate and enhance this collaborative structure, the government has designated a "Lead Agency" for each of the major sectors of the economy vulnerable to infrastructure attack. In addition, the Office of Science and Technology Policy (OSTP) coordinates research and development to support critical infrastructure protection. The Office of Management and Budget (OMB) oversees the implementation of governmentwide policies, principles, standards, and guidelines for federal government computer security programs. The Department of State coordinates international outreach on cybersecurity. The Director of Central Intelligence is responsible for assessing the foreign threat to U.S. networks and information systems. The Department of Justice (DOJ) and the Federal Bureau of Investigation (FBI) lead the national effort to investigate and prosecute cybercrime.

The government will continue to support the development of public-private partnerships. Working together, sector representatives and federal lead agencies assess their respective sectors' vulnerabilities to cyber or physical attacks and, accordingly, recommend plans or measures to eliminate significant exposures. Both technology and the threat environment can change rapidly. Therefore, sectors and lead agencies should frequently assess the reliability, vulnerability, and threat environments of the Nation's infrastructures and employ appropriate protective measures and responses to safeguard them.

The government's full authority, capabilities, and resources must be available to support critical infrastructure protection efforts. These include, as appropriate, crisis management, law enforcement, regulation, foreign intelligence, and defense preparedness.

Priority I: A National Cyberspace Security Response System

In the 1950s and 1960s, our Nation became vulnerable to attacks from aircraft and missiles for the first time. The federal government responded by creating a national system to: monitor our airspace with radar to detect unusual activity, analyze and warn of possible attacks, coordinate our fighter aircraft defenses during an attack, and restore our Nation after an attack through civil defense programs.

Today, the Nation's critical assets could be attacked through cyberspace. The United States now requires a different kind of national response system in order to detect potentially damaging activity in cyberspace, to analyze exploits and warn potential victims, to

coordinate incident responses, and to restore essential services that have been damaged.

The fact that the vast majority of cyberspace is neither owned nor operated by any single group —public or private—presents a challenge for creating a National Cyberspace Security Response System. There is no synoptic or holistic view of cyberspace. Therefore, there is no panoramic vantage point from which we can see attacks coming or spreading. Information that indicates an attack has occurred (worms, viruses, denial-of-service attacks) accumulates through many different organizations. However, there is no organized mechanism for reviewing these indicators and determining their implications.

To mitigate the impact of cyber attacks, information about them must disseminate widely and quickly. Analytical and incident response capabilities that exist in numerous organizations could be coordinated to determine how to best defend against an attack, mitigate effects, and restore service.

Establishing a proper administrative mechanism for the National Cyberspace Security Response System presents another challenge. Unlike the U.S. airspace-monitoring program during the Cold War, individuals who operate the systems that enable and protect cyberspace usually are not federal employees. Thus, the National Cyberspace Security Response System must operate from a less formal, collaborative network of governmental and nongovernmental organizations.

DHS is responsible for developing the national cyberspace security response system, which includes:

- Providing crisis management support in response to threats to, or attacks on, critical information systems; and

- Coordinating with other agencies of the federal government to provide specific warning information, and advice about appropriate protective measures and countermeasures, to state and local government agencies and authorities, the private sector, other entities, and the public.

DHS will lead and synchronize efforts for the National Cyberspace Security Response System as part of its overall information sharing and crisis coordination mandate; however, the system itself will consist of many organizations from both government and private sectors. The authorizing legislation for the Department of Homeland Security also created the position of a privacy officer to ensure that any mechanisms

The National Cyberspace Security Response System

The National Cyberspace Security Response System is a public-private architecture, coordinated by the Department of Homeland Security, for analyzing and warning; managing incidents of national significance; promoting continuity in government systems and private sector infrastructures; and increasing information sharing across and between organizations to improve cyberspace security. The National Cyberspace Security Response System will include governmental entities and nongovernmental entities, such as private sector information sharing and analysis centers (ISACs).

associated with the National Cyberspace Security Response System appropriately balance its mission with civil liberty and privacy concerns. This officer will consult regularly with privacy advocates, industry experts, and the public at large to ensure broad input and consideration of privacy issues so that we achieve solutions that protect privacy while enhancing security.

Among the system components outlined below are existing federal programs and new federal initiatives pending budget-review consideration, as well as initiatives recommended for our partners.

A. ESTABLISH PUBLIC-PRIVATE ARCHITECTURE FOR RESPONDING TO NATIONAL-LEVEL CYBER INCIDENTS

Establishing the National Cyberspace Security Response System will not require an expensive or bureaucratic federal program. In many cases the system will augment the capabilities of several important federal entities with existing cyberspace security responsibilities, which are

National Cyberspace Security Response System

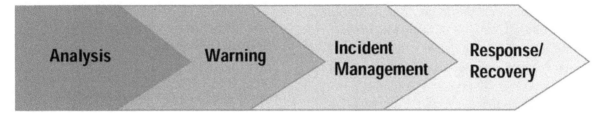

Components/ Capabilities

DHS Analysis Center	DHS Incident Operations Center	DHS Incident Management Structure	National Response Contingency Plans
• Strategic group • Tactical group • Vulnerability assessments	• Cyber Warning and Information Network • ISACs	• Federal coordination • Private, state and local coordination	• Federal plans • Private plan coordination

now part of DHS. The synergy that results from integrating the resources of the National Communications System, the National Infrastructure Protection Center's analysis and warning functions, the Federal Computer Incident Response Center, the Office of Energy Assurance, and the Critical Infrastructure Assurance Office under the purview of the Under Secretary for Information Analysis and Infrastructure Protection will help build the necessary foundation for the National Cyberspace Security Response System.

The Nation's private-sector networks are increasingly targeted, and they will therefore likely be the first organizations to detect attacks with potential national significance. Thus, ISACs will play an increasingly important role in the National Cyberspace Security Response System and the overall missions of homeland security. ISACs possess unique operational insight into their industries' core functions and will help provide the necessary analysis to support national efforts.

Typically, an ISAC is an industry-led mechanism for gathering, analyzing, sanitizing, and disseminating sector-specific security infor- mation and articulating and promulgating best

practices. ISACs are designed by the various sectors to meet their respective needs and financed through their memberships. DHS will work closely with ISACs as appropriate to ensure that they receive timely and actionable threat and vulnerability data and to coordinate voluntary contingency planning efforts. The federal government encourages the private sector to continue to establish ISACs and, further, to enhance the analytical capabilities of existing ISACs.

1. Analysis

a. Provide for the Development of Tactical and Strategic Analysis of Cyber Attacks and Vulnerability Assessments

Analysis is the first step toward gaining important insight about a cyber incident, including the nature of attack, the information it compromised, and the extent of damage it caused. Analysis can also provide an indication of the intruder's possible intentions, the potential tools he used, and the vulnerabilities he exploited. There are three closely related, but discrete, categories of analysis related to cyberspace:

(i) Tactical analysis examines factors associated with incidents under investigation or specific, identified vulnerabilities to generate indications and warnings. Examples of tactical analysis include: examining the delivery mechanism of a computer virus to develop and issue immediate guidance on ways to prevent or mitigate damage; and studying a specific computer intrusion, or set of intrusions, to determine the perpetrator, his motive, and his method of attack.

(ii) Strategic analysis looks beyond specific incidents to consider broader sets of incidents or implications that may indicate threats of potential national importance. For example, strategic analyses may identify long-term trends related to threat and vulnerability that could be used to provide advanced warnings of increasing risks, such as emerging attack methods. Strategic analysis also provides policymakers with information they can use to anticipate and prepare for attacks, thereby diminishing the damage they cause. Strategic analysis also provides a foundation to identify patterns that can support indications and warnings.

(iii) Vulnerability assessments are detailed reviews of cyber systems and their physical components to identify and study their weaknesses. Vulnerability assessments are an integral part of the intelligence cycle for cyberspace security. These assessments enable planners to predict the consequences of possible cyber attacks against specific facilities or sectors of the economy or government. These projections then allow infrastructure owners and operators to strengthen their defenses against various types of threat. (This will be discussed in the *Cyberspace Security Threat and Vulnerability Reduction Program.*)

DHS will foster the development of strong analytic capabilities in each of these areas. It should seek partnership and assistance from the private sector, including the ISACs, in developing these capabilities.

2. Warning

a. Encourage the Development of a Private Sector Capability to Share a Synoptic View of the Health of Cyberspace

The lack of a synoptic view of the Internet frustrates efforts to develop Internet threat analysis and indication and warning capabilities. The effects of a cyber attack on one sector have the potential to cascade across several other sectors, thereby producing significant consequences that could rapidly overwhelm the capabilities of many private companies and state and local governments. DHS's integration of several key federal cybersecurity operations centers creates a focal point for the federal government to manage cybersecurity emergencies in its own systems, and, if requested, facilitate crisis management in non-federal critical infrastructure systems.

Separately, industry is encouraged to develop a mechanism—whether virtual or physical—that could enable the sharing of aggregated information on Internet health to improve analysis, warning, response, and recovery. To the extent permitted by law, this voluntary coordination of activities among nongovernmental entities could enable different network operators and Internet backbone providers to analyze and exchange data about attacks. Such coordination could prevent exploits from escalating and causing damage or disruption of vital systems.

DHS will create a single point-of-contact for the federal government's interaction with industry and other partners for 24 x7 functions, including cyberspace analysis, warning, information sharing, major incident response, and national-level recovery efforts. Private sector organizations, which have major contributions for those functions, are encouraged to coordinate activities, as permitted by law, in order to provide a synoptic view of the health of cyberspace on a 24 x 7 basis. (A/R 1-1)

b. Expand the Cyber Warning and Information Network to Support DHS's Role in Coordinating Crisis Management for Cyberspace

Hours and minutes can make a difference between a major disruption and a manageable incident. Improving national capabilities for warning requires a secure infrastructure to provide assured communications between critical asset owners and operators and their service providers. The Cyber Warning and Information Network (CWIN) will provide an out-of-band private and secure communications network for government and industry, with the purpose of sharing cyber alert and warning information. The network will include voice conferencing and data collaboration.

While the first phase was implemented between the federal government cyber watch centers, CWIN participants will ultimately include other critical government and industry partners, such as ISACs that deal with cyber threats on a daily basis. As other entities expand in this area, membership will increase as well. Key to CWIN membership is the ability to share sensitive cyber threat information in a secure, protected, and trusted environment.

As outlined in the 2003 budget, the federal government will complete the installation of CWIN to key government cybersecurity-related network operation centers, to disseminate analysis and warning information and perform crisis coordination. The federal government will also explore linking the ISACs to CWIN. (A/R 1-2)

3. National Incident Management

Enhancing analytical capabilities within DHS, the private sector ISACs, and expanding CWIN will contribute to the improvement of national cyber incident management. However, incident management within the federal government will still require coordination with organizations other than those being transferred to DHS. For example, the Departments of

Justice, Defense, and Commerce all have roles to perform in response to incidents in cyberspace. Within the White House a number offices have responsibilities, including the Office of Science and Technology Policy, which is responsible for executing emergency telecommunications authorities, the National Security Council, which coordinates all matters related to national security and international cooperation, and the Office of Management and Budget.

In addition, national incident management capabilities will also integrate state chief information officers as well as international entities, as appropriate. (See, *Priorities IV and V.*)

4. Response and Recovery

a. Create Processes to Coordinate the Voluntary Development of National Public-Private Continuity and Contingency Plans

Among the lessons learned from security reviews following the events of September 11, 2001, was that federal agencies had vastly inconsistent, and in most cases incomplete, contingency capabilities for their communications and other systems. Contingency planning is a key element of cybersecurity. Without adequate contingency planning and training, agencies may not be able to effectively handle disruptions in service and ensure business continuity. OMB, through the Federal Information Security Management Act requirements and with assistance from the inspectors general, is holding agencies accountable for developing continuity plans.

b. Exercise Cybersecurity Continuity Plans in Federal Cyber Systems

DHS has the responsibility for providing crisis management support in response to threats to, or attacks on, critical information systems for other government agencies, state and local governments and, upon request, the private sector. In order to establish a baseline understanding of federal readiness, DHS will explore exercises for the civilian agencies similar to the Defense Department "Eligible Receiver" exercises that test cybersecurity preparedness.

To test civilian agencies' security preparedness and contingency planning, DHS will use exercises to evaluate the impact of cyber attacks on governmentwide processes. Weaknesses discovered will be included in agency corrective action plans and submitted to OMB. DHS also will explore such exercises as a way to test the coordination of public and private incident management, response and recovery capabilities. (A/R 1-3)

(i) Encourage increased cyber risk management and business continuity. There are a number of measures that nongovernmental entities can employ to manage the risk posed by cyberspace and plan for business continuity. Risk management is a discipline that involves risk assessment, risk prevention, risk mitigation, risk transfer, and risk retention.

There is no special technology that can make an enterprise completely secure. No matter how much money companies spend on cybersecurity, they may not be able to prevent disruptions caused by organized attackers. Some businesses whose products or services directly or indirectly impact the economy or the health, welfare or safety of the public have begun to use cyber risk insurance programs as a means of transferring risk and providing for business continuity.

An important way to reduce an organization's exposure to cyber-related losses, as well as to help protect companies from operational and financial impairment, is to ensure that adequate contingency plans are developed and tested.

Corporations are encouraged to regularly review and exercise IT continuity plans and to consider diversity in IT service providers as a way of mitigating risk. (A/R 1-4)

(ii) Promote public-private contingency planning for cybersecurity. It may not be possible to prevent a wide-range of cyber attacks. For those attacks that do occur, the Nation needs an integrated public-private plan for responding to significant outages or disruptions in cyberspace. Some organizations have plans for how they will recover their cyber network and capabilities in the event of a major outage or catastrophe. However, there is no mechanism for coordinating such plans across an entire infrastructure or at a national level.

The legislation establishing DHS also provides a trusted mechanism for private industry to develop contingency planning by using the voluntary preparedness planning provisions that were established in the Defense Production Act of 1950, as amended.

Infrastructure sectors are encouraged to establish mutual assistance programs for cybersecurity emergencies. DoJ and the Federal Trade Commission should work with the sectors to address barriers to such cooperation, as appropriate. In addition, DHS's Information Analysis and Infrastructure Protection Directorate will coordinate the development and regular update of voluntary, joint government-industry cybersecurity contingency plans, including a plan for recovering Internet functions. (A/R 1-5)

B. INFORMATION SHARING

1. Improve and Enhance Public-Private Information Sharing about Cyber Attacks, Threats, and Vulnerabilities

Successfully developing capabilities for analysis, indications, and warnings requires a voluntary public-private information sharing effort. The voluntary sharing of information about such incidents or attacks is vital to cybersecurity. Real or perceived legal obstacles make some organizations hesitant to share information about cyber incidents with the government or with each other. First, some fear that shared data that is confidential, proprietary, or potentially embarrassing could become subject to public examination when shared with the government. Second, concerns about competitive advantage may impede information sharing between companies within an industry. Finally, in some cases, the mechanisms are simply not yet in place to allow efficient sharing of information.

The legislation establishing DHS provides several specific mechanisms intended to improve two-way information sharing. First, the legislation encourages industry to share information with DHS by ensuring that such voluntarily provided data about threats and vulnerabilities will not be disclosed in a manner that could damage the submitter. Second, the legislation requires that the federal government share information and analysis with the private sector as appropriate and consistent with the need to protect classified and other sensitive national security information.

As required by law, DHS, in consultation with appropriate federal agencies, will establish uniform procedures for the receipt, care, and storage by federal agencies of critical infrastructure information that is voluntarily submitted to the government.

The procedures will address how the Department will:

- Acknowledge the receipt of voluntarily submitted critical infrastructure information;

- Maintain the information as voluntarily submitted critical infrastructure information;

- Establish protocols for the care and storage of such information; and

- Create methods for protecting the confidentiality of the submitting entity while still allowing the information to be used in the issuance of notices and warnings for protection of the critical infrastructure.

DHS will raise awareness about the removal of impediments to information sharing about cybersecurity and infrastructure vulnerabilities between the public and private sectors. The Department will also establish an infrastructure protection program office to manage the information flow, including the development of protocols for how to care for "voluntarily submitted critical infrastructure information." (A/R 1-6)

2. Encourage Broader Information Sharing on Cybersecurity

Nongovernmental organizations with significant computing resources are encouraged to take active roles in information sharing organizations. Corporations, colleges, and universities can play important roles in detecting and reporting cyber attacks, exploits, or vulnerabilities. In particular, both corporations and institutions of higher learning can gain from increased sharing on cyberspace security issues. Programs such as ISACs, FBI Infragard, or the United States Secret Service electronic crimes task forces can also benefit the respective participants. Because institutions of higher learning have vast computer resources that can be used as launch pads for attacks, colleges and universities are encouraged to consider establishing an on-call point-of-contact to Internet service providers (ISPs) and law enforcement officials.

Corporations are encouraged to consider active involvement in industrywide programs to share information on IT security, including the potential benefits of joining an appropriate ISAC. Colleges and universities are encouraged to consider establishing: (1) one or more ISACs to deal with cyber attacks and vulnerabilities; and, (2) an on-call point-of-contact, to Internet service providers and law enforcement officials in the event that the school's IT systems are discovered to be launching cyber attacks. (A/R 1-7)

Priority II: A National Cyberspace Security Threat and Vulnerability Reduction Program

Malicious actors in cyberspace can take many forms including individuals, criminal cartels, terrorists, or nation states. While attackers take many forms, they all seek to exploit vulnerabilities created by the design or implementation of software, hardware, networks, and protocols to achieve a wide range of political or economic effects. As our reliance on cyberspace increases so too does the scope of damage that malicious actors can impose.

Waiting to act until we learn that a malicious actor is about to exploit a particular vulnera-

bility is risky. Such warning information may not always be available. Even when warning data is available, remediation of some vulnerabilities may take days, weeks, or even years. As a result, vulnerabilities must be identified and corrected in critical networks before threats surface. The most dangerous vulnerabilities must be prioritized and reduced in a systematic fashion.

As technology evolves and new systems are introduced, new vulnerabilities emerge. Our strategy cannot be to eliminate all vulnerabilities, or to deter all threats. Rather, we will pursue a three-part effort to:

(1) Reduce threats and deter malicious actors through effective programs to identify and punish them;

(2) Identify and remediate those existing vulnerabilities that could create the most damage to critical systems, if exploited; and

(3) Develop new systems with less vulnerability and assess emerging technologies for vulnerabilities.

The federal government cannot accomplish these goals acting alone. It can only do so in partnership with state and local governments and the private sector. Many federal agencies must play a part in this effort, which will be led and coordinated by DHS as part of its overall vulnerability reduction mandate.

The components of this program are discussed in this section. They include federal programs (both existing programs and initiatives that will be considered as part of the budget decision making process) and activities that the federal government recommends to its partners. Many activities that can be taken by individuals, companies, and other private organizations to reduce vulnerabilities will be stimulated and accelerated through awareness and are discussed as part of the awareness initiative described in Priority III.

A. REDUCE THREAT AND DETER MALICIOUS ACTORS

1. Enhance Law Enforcement's Capabilities for Preventing and Prosecuting

The *National Strategy to Secure Cyberspace* is especially concerned with those threats that could cause significant damage to our economy or security through actions taken using or against our cyber infrastructure. By identifying threats that would cause us significant harm, we can reduce the threats to homeland security, national security, and the economy. Law enforcement and the national security community play a critical role in preventing attacks in cyberspace. Law enforcement plays the central role in attributing an attack through the exercise of criminal justice authorities.

Many cyber-based attacks are crimes. As a result the Justice Department's Computer Crime and Intellectual Property Section, the FBI's Cyber Division, and the U.S. Secret Service all play a central role in apprehending and swiftly bringing to justice the responsible individuals. When incidents do occur, a rapid response can stem the tide of an ongoing attack and lessen the harm that is ultimately caused. The Nation currently has laws and mechanisms to ensure quick responses to large incidents. Ideally, an investigation, arrest, and prosecution of the perpetrators, or a diplomatic or military response in the case of a state-sponsored action, will follow such an incident.

Threat reduction, however, involves more than prosecution. Analyzing and disseminating practical information gathered by law enforcement can help promote national infrastructure security. For example, through various initiatives such as the FBI Infragard program and the U.S. Secret Service electronic crimes task forces, law enforcement can share lessons learned from attacks with private sector organizations. The information gleaned from investigations can provide the federal government and private industry a framework for examining the robustness of their cybersecurity skill sets, and assist in prioritizing their limited resources to manage the unique risk of their enterprise.

Justice and the FBI will need to work closely with DHS to ensure that the information gleaned from investigations is appropriately analyzed and shared with ISACs and other nongovernmental entities to promote improved risk management in critical infrastructure sectors.

The Nation will seek to prevent, deter, and significantly reduce cyber attacks by ensuring the identification of actual or attempted perpetrators followed by an appropriate government response. In the case of cybercrime this would include swift apprehension, and appropriately severe punishment.

DOJ and other appropriate agencies will develop and implement efforts to reduce cyber attacks and cyber threats through the following means: (1) identifying ways to improve information sharing and investigative coordination within the federal, state, and local law enforcement community working on critical infrastructure and cyberspace security matters, and with other agencies and the private sector; (2) exploring means to provide sufficient investigative and forensic resources and training to facilitate expeditious investigation and resolution of critical infrastructure incidents; and, (3) developing better data about victims of cybercrime and intrusions in order to understand the scope of the problem and be able to track changes over time. (A/R 2-1)

2. Create a Process for National Vulnerability Assessments to Better Understand the Potential Consequences of Threats and Vulnerabilities

a. Assess the Potential Impact of Strategic Cyber Attacks

To better understand how to further detect and prevent attacks, the Nation must know the threat it is facing. To date, no comprehensive assessment of the impact of a strategic cyber attack against the United States has been conducted. Because nation states and terrorists are developing capabilities for cyber-based attacks, it is important to understand the potential impact of such an attack and possible ways to mitigate the effects. *DHS, in coordination with appropriate agencies and the private sector, will lead in the development and conduct of a national threat assessment including red teaming, blue teaming, and other methods to identify the*

impact of possible attacks on a variety of targets. (A/R 2-2)

B. IDENTIFY AND REMEDIATE EXISTING VULNERABILITIES

Reducing vulnerabilities can be resource intensive. Accordingly, our national efforts to identify and remediate vulnerabilities must be focused to reduce vulnerabilities in a cost effective and systematic manner. The United States must reduce vulnerabilities in four major components of cyberspace, including: (1) the mechanisms of the Internet; (2) digital control

How the Internet Works

Data sent from one computer to another across the Internet is broken into small packets of information containing addressing information as well as a portion of the total message. The packets travel across the Internet separately and are reassembled at the receiving computer. There are two primary protocols that enable these packets of data to traverse the complex networks and arrive in an understandable format. These protocols are: (1) the Transmission Control Protocol (TCP) which decomposes data into packets and ensures that they are reassembled properly at the destination; and (2) the Internet Protocol (IP), which guides or routes the packets of data though the Internet. Together they are referred to as TCP/IP.

IP is essential to almost all Internet activities including sending data such as e-mail. Data is transmitted based on IP addresses, which are a series of numbers. The Domain Name System (DNS) was developed to simplify the management of IP addresses. The DNS maps IP numbers to recognizable sets of letters, words or numbers. The DNS does this by establishing domains and a structured hierarchical addressing scheme.

systems/supervisory control and data acquisition systems; (3) software and hardware vulnerability remediation; and, (4) physical infrastructure and interdependency. These four areas have broad implications for the majority of the Nation's critical infrastructures. Initiating efforts to eliminate vulnerabilities in these important areas will reduce the vulnerability of critical infrastructure services to attack or compromise.

1. Secure the Mechanisms of the Internet

The development and implementation of the mechanisms for securing the Internet are responsibilities shared by its owners, operators, and users. Private industry is leading the effort to ensure that the core functions of the Internet develop in a secure manner. As appropriate, the federal government will continue to support these efforts. The goal is the development of secure and robust mechanisms that will enable the Internet to support the Nation's needs now and in the future. This will include securing the protocols on which the Internet is based, ensuring the security of the routers that direct the flow of data, and implementing effective management practices.

a. Improve the Security and Resilience of Key Internet Protocols

Essential to the security of the Internet infrastructure is ensuring the reliability and secure use of three key protocols: the Internet Protocol (IP), the Domain Name System (DNS), and the Border Gateway Protocol (BGP).

(i) Internet Protocol. The Internet is currently based on Internet Protocol version 4 (IPv4). Some organizations and countries are moving to an updated version of the protocol, version 6 (IPv6). IPv6 offers several advantages over IPv4. In addition to offering a vast amount of addresses, it provides for improved security features, including attribution and native IP security (IPSEC), as well as enabling new applications and capabilities. Some countries are moving aggressively to adopt IPv6. Japan has

committed to a fully IPv6 based infrastructure by 2005. The European Union has initiated steps to move to IPv6. China is also considering early adoption of the protocol.

The United States must understand the merits of, and obstacles to, moving to IPv6 and, based on that understanding, identify a process for moving to an IPv6 based infrastructure. The federal government can lead in developing this understanding by employing IPv6 on some of its own networks and by coordinating its activities with those in the private sector. *The Department of Commerce will form a task force to examine the issues related to IPv6, including the appropriate role of government, international interoperability, security in transition, and costs and benefits. The task force will solicit input from potentially impacted industry segments. (A/R 2-3).*

(ii) Secure the Domain Name System. DNS serves as the central database that helps route information throughout the Internet. The ability to route information can be disrupted when the databases cannot be accessed or updated or when they have been corrupted. Attackers can disrupt the DNS by flooding the system with information or requests or by gaining access to the system and corrupting or destroying the information that it contains. The October 21, 2002 attacks on the core DNS root servers revealed a vulnerability of the Internet by degrading or disrupting some of the 13 root servers necessary for the DNS to function. The occurrence of this attack punctuates the urgent need for expeditious action to make such attacks more difficult and less effective.

(iii) Border Gateway Protocol. Of the many routing protocols in use within the Internet, the Border Gateway Protocol (BGP) is at greatest risk of being the target of attacks designed to disrupt or degrade service on a large scale. BGP is used to interconnect the thousands of networks that make up the Internet. It allows routing information to be exchanged between networks that may have separate administrators, administrative policies, or protocols.

Propagation of false routing information in the Internet can deny service to small or large portions of the Internet. For example, false routes can create "black holes" that absorb traffic destined for a particular block of address space. They can also lead to cascade failures that have occurred in other types of large routing/switching systems in the past, where the failure of one switch or mechanism results in the failure of those connected to it, resulting in additional waves of failures expanding outward from the initial fault.

More secure forms of BGP and DNS will benefit all owners, operators and users of the Internet. To address this issue, the Internet Engineering Task Force, a voluntary private body consisting of users, owners, and operators of the Internet, has established working groups for securing BGP and DNS. These groups have made progress, but have been limited by technical obstacles and the need for coordination.

The security and continued functioning of the Internet will be greatly influenced by the success or failure of implementing more secure and more robust BGP and DNS. The Nation has a vital interest in ensuring that this work proceeds. The government should play a role when private efforts break down due to a need for coordination or a lack of proper incentives.

b. Promote Improved Internet Routing

Routers on the Internet share a number of design characteristics that make them relatively easy to disable, especially through denial-of-service (DoS) attacks that overwhelm a router's processing capability. Internet routing can be substantially improved by promoting increased use of address verification and "out-of-band" management.

(i) Address Verification. Today there are few effective solutions available, even commercially, to mitigate the effect of DoS attacks, as the scale and lack of address verification and accountability makes filtering and contacting the sources of an attack impossible. One of the largest weaknesses in our current Internet infrastructure is the lack of source address verification. Establishing an Internet infrastructure that provides forged source address filtering is a critical step towards defeating these types of attacks.

(ii) Out-of-Band Management. DoS attacks are difficult to mitigate because they prevent control data from reaching the router. Separate control networks, commonly called "out-of-band" management links, are one technique that can be used to counter DoS attacks.

DHS will examine the need for increased research to improve router security through new technology or approaches to routing information. In particular, DHS will assess progress on out-of-band management and address filtering and recommend steps that can be taken by government or the private sector to improve their effectiveness and use. In addition, DHS will work with the private sector to understand the most efficient path and obstacles to increasing router security using current techniques and technology.

c. Improve Management

Much improvement can be made in the security of the Internet infrastructure if best practices for managing the Internet, including the data that flows through it and the equipment that supports it, are widely employed. DHS will work with organizations that own and operate the Internet to develop and promote the adoption of best practices. In particular, DHS will work with Internet service providers to help develop a widely accepted "code of conduct" for network management. This work will include a review of existing documented best practices such as those published by Network Reliability and Interoperability Council (NRIC) of the Federal Communications Commission (FCC).

DHS, in coordination with the Commerce Department and appropriate agencies, will coordinate public-private partnerships to encourage: (1) the adoption of improved security protocols; (2) the development of more secure router technology; and, (3) the adoption by ISPs of a "code of good conduct," including cybersecurity practices and security related cooperation. DHS will support these efforts as required for their success, subject to other budget considerations. (A/R 2-4)

2. Foster Trusted Digital Control Systems / Supervisory Control and Data Acquisition Systems

Many industries in America have radically transformed the way they control and monitor equipment over the last 20 years by employing digital control systems (DCS) and supervisory control and data acquisition systems (SCADA). DCS/SCADA are computer-based systems that are used by many infrastructures and industries to remotely control sensitive processes and physical functions that once had to be controlled manually. DCS and SCADA are present in almost every sector of the economy including water, transportation, chemicals, energy, and manufacturing, among others. Increasingly DCS/SCADA systems use the Internet to transmit data rather than the closed networks used in the past.

Securing DCS/SCADA is a national priority. Disruption of these systems can have significant consequences for public health and safety. However, securing these systems is complicated by various factors. First, adding security requires investment in systems and in research and development that companies cannot afford or justify on their own. Such research may require the involvement of multiple infrastructure operators or industries. Second, current technological limitations could impede the implementation of security measures. For example, DCS/SCADA systems are typically small and self-contained units with limited power supplies. Security features are not easily adapted to the space or power requirements. In

addition, these systems operate in real time and security measures could reduce performance or impact the synchronization of larger processes.

Both the private and public sectors have a role in securing SCADA systems. DHS, in coordination with the Department of Energy and other concerned agencies, will work in partnership with private industry to ensure that there is broad awareness among industry vendors and users, both regulated and unregulated, of the vulnerabilities in DCS/SCADA systems, and the consequences of exploitation of those vulnerabilities. For operators of DCS/SCADA systems, these efforts should include developing and deploying training and certification of DCS/SCADA-oriented software and hardware security. In addition, DHS will work with the private sector to promote voluntary standards efforts, and security policy creation.

The development of adequate test bed environments and the development of technology in the areas of extremely low latency link encryptors/authenticators, key management, and network status/state-of-health monitoring will aid in the effort to secure DCS/SCADA. *DHS, in coordination with DOE and other concerned agencies and in partnership with industry, will develop best practices and new technology to increase security of DCS/SCADA, to determine the most critical DCS/SCADA-related sites, and to develop a prioritized plan for short-term cybersecurity improvements in those sites. (A/R 2-5)*

3. Reduce and Remediate Software Vulnerabilities

A third critical area of national exposure is the many flaws that exist in critical infrastructure due to software vulnerabilities. New vulnerabilities emerge daily as use of software reveals flaws that malicious actors can exploit. Currently, approximately 3,500 vulnerabilities are reported annually. Corrections are usually completed by the manufacturer in the form of a patch and made available for distribution to fix the flaws.

Many known flaws, for which solutions are available, remain uncorrected for long periods of time. For example, the top ten known vulnerabilities account for the majority of reported incidents of cyber attacks. This happens for multiple reasons. Many system administrators may lack adequate training or may not have time to examine every new patch to determine whether it applies to their system. The software to be patched may affect a complex set of interconnected systems that take a long time to test before a patch can be installed with confidence. If the systems are critical, it could be difficult to shut them down to install the patch.

Unpatched software in critical infrastructures makes those infrastructures vulnerable to penetration and exploitation. Software flaws are exploited to propagate "worms" that can result in denial of service, disruption, or other serious damage. Such flaws can be used to gain access to and control over physical infrastructure. Improving the speed, coverage, and effectiveness of remediation of these vulnerabilities is important for both the public and private sector.

Several steps will help. First, the Nation needs a better-defined approach to the disclosure of vulnerabilities. The issue is complex because exposing vulnerabilities both helps speed the development of solutions and also creates opportunities for would be attackers. In addition, the clearinghouse for such disclosures must be a neutral body between vendors, security companies, and the public at large. Today the government partially funds such organizations. However, the appropriate level and form for this funding need to be reviewed. *DHS will work with the National Infrastructure Advisory Council and private sector organizations to develop an optimal approach and mechanism for vulnerability disclosure. (A/R 2-6)*

A second step that will speed the distribution of patches in software systems is the creation of common test-beds. Such test-beds running applications that are common among government agencies or companies can speed patch implementation by testing one time, for many users, the impact that a patch will have on a variety of applications. *GSA will work with DHS on an improved approach to implementing a patch clearinghouse for the federal government. DHS will also share lessons learned with the private sector and encourage the development of a voluntary, industry-led, national effort to develop a similar clearinghouse for other sectors including large enterprises. (A/R 2-7)*

Finally, best practices in vulnerability remediation should be established and shared in areas such as training requirements for system administrators, the use of automated tools, and management processes for patch implementation. DHS will work with public and private entities on the development and dissemination of such practices. More secure initial configurations for shipped cyber products would facilitate more secure use by making the default set-up secure rather than insecure. *The software industry is encouraged to consider promoting more secure "out-of-the-box" installation and implementation of their products, including increasing: (1) user awareness of the security features in products; (2) ease-of-use for security functions; and, (3) where feasible, promotion of industry guidelines and best practices that support such efforts. (A/R 2-8)*

4. Understand Infrastructure Interdependency and Improve Physical Security of Cyber Systems and Telecommunications

Reducing the vulnerability of the cyber infrastructure includes mitigating the potentially devastating attacks on cyberspace that can occur when key physical linkages are destroyed. The impact of such attacks can be amplified by cascading impacts through a variety of dependant infrastructures affecting both the economy and the health and welfare of citizens: a train derailed in a Baltimore tunnel and the

Internet slowed in Chicago; a campfire in New Mexico damaged a gas pipeline and IT-related production halted in Silicon Valley; a satellite spun out of control hundreds of miles above the Earth and affected bank customers could not use their ATMs.

Cyberspace has physical manifestations: the buildings and conduits that support telecommunications and Internet networks. These physical elements have been designed and built to create redundancy and avoid single points of failure. Nonetheless, the carriers and service providers are encouraged to independently and collectively continue to analyze their networks to strengthen reliability and intentional redundancy. The FCC, through its Network Reliability and Interoperability Council, and the National Security Telecommunications Advisory Committee, can contribute to such efforts and should identify any governmental impediments to strengthening the national networks.

DHS will work actively to reduce interdependencies and physical vulnerability. *DHS will establish and lead a public-private partnership to identify cross-sectoral interdependencies, both cyber and physical. The partnership will develop plans to reduce related vulnerabilities in conjunction with programs proposed in the National Strategy for Homeland Security. The National Infrastructure Simulation and Analysis Center in DHS will support these efforts by developing models to identify the impact of cyber and physical interdependencies. (A/R 2-9)*

DHS also will support, when requested and as appropriate, voluntary efforts by owners and operators of information system networks and network data centers to develop remediation and contingency plans to reduce the consequences of large-scale physical damage to facilities supporting such networks, and to develop appropriate procedures for limiting access to critical facilities. (A/R 2-10)

C. DEVELOP SYSTEMS WITH FEWER VULNERABILITIES AND ASSESS EMERGING TECHNOLOGIES FOR VULNERABILITIES

As the Nation takes steps to improve the security of current systems, it must also ensure that future cyber systems and infrastructure are built to be secure. This will become increasingly important as more and more of our daily economic and physical lives come to depend on cyber infrastructure. Future security requires research in cyberspace security topics and a commitment to the development of more secure products.

1. Prioritize the Federal Research and Development Agenda

Federal investment in research for the next generation of technologies to maintain and secure cyberspace must keep pace with an increasing number of vulnerabilities. Flexibility and nimbleness are important in ensuring that the research and development process accommodates the dynamic technology environment in the years ahead.

The Nation will prioritize and provide resources as necessary to advance the research to secure cyberspace. A new generation of enabling technologies will serve to "modernize" the Internet for rapidly growing traffic volumes, expanded e-commerce, and the advanced applications that will be possible only when next-generation networks are widely available. As a result, national research efforts must be prioritized to support the transition of cyberspace into a secure, high-speed knowledge and communications infrastructure for this century. Vital research is required for this effort. The Nation must prioritize its cyberspace security research efforts across all sectors and funding sources.

To meet these needs, the Director of OSTP will coordinate the development, and update on an annual basis, a federal government research and development agenda that includes near-term (1-3 years), mid-term (3-5 years), and later (5 years out and longer) IT security research for Fiscal Year 2004 and beyond. Existing priorities include, among others, intrusion detection, Internet infrastructure security (including protocols such as BGP and DNS), application security, DoS, communications security (including SCADA system encryption and authentication), high-assurance systems, and secure system composition. (A/R 2-11)

To optimize research efforts relative to those of the private sector, DHS will ensure that adequate mechanisms exist for coordination of research and development among academia, industry, and government, and will develop new mechanisms where needed. (A/R 2-12)

An important goal of cybersecurity research will be the development of highly secure, trustworthy, and resilient computing systems. In the future, working with a computer, the Internet, or any other cyber system may become as dependable as turning on the lights or the water.

The Nation must seek to ensure that future components of the cyber infrastructure are built to be inherently secure and dependable for their users. Development of highly secure and reliable systems will be pursued, subject to budgeting constraints, through the national cyberspace security research agenda.

The private sector is encouraged to consider including in near-term research and development priorities, programs for highly secure and trustworthy operating systems. If such systems are developed and successfully evaluated, the federal government will, subject to budget considerations, accelerate procurement of such systems. (A/R 2-13)

In addition, DHS will facilitate a national public-private effort to promulgate best practices and methodologies that promote integrity, security, and reliability in software code development, including

processes and procedures that diminish the possibilities of erroneous code, malicious code, or trap doors that could be introduced during development. (A/R 2-14)

2. Assess and Secure Emerging Systems

As new technologies are developed they introduce the potential for new security vulnerabilities. Some new technologies introduce security weaknesses that are only corrected over time, with great difficulty, or sometimes not at all. A person driving in a car around a city, for example, can access many wireless local area networks without the knowledge of their owners unless strong security measures are added to those systems.

As telephones and personal digital assistants, and many other mobile devices, incorporate more sophisticated operating systems and connectivity they may require security features to prevent their exploitation for distributed attacks on mobile networks and even the Internet.

Emerging areas of research also can produce unforeseen consequences for security. The emergence of optical computing and intelligent agents, as well as in the longer term, developments in areas such as nanotechnology and quantum computing, among others, will likely reshape cyberspace and its security. The Nation must be at the leading edge in understanding these technologies and their implications for security.

DHS, in coordination with OSTP and other agencies, as appropriate, will facilitate communication between the public and private research and the security communities, to ensure that emerging technologies are periodically reviewed by the appropriate body within the National Science and Technology Council, in the context of possible homeland and cyberspace security implications, and relevance to the federal research agenda. (A/R 2-15)

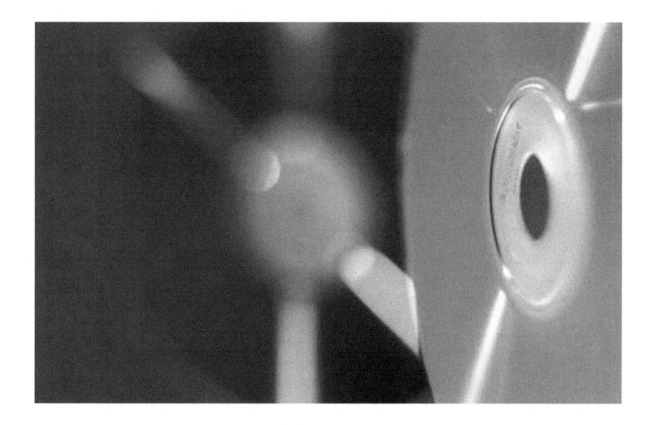

Priority III: A National Cyberspace Security Awareness and Training Program

Everyone who relies on part of cyberspace is encouraged to help secure the part of cyberspace that they can influence or control.

To do that, users need to know the simple things that they can do to help to prevent intrusions, cyber attacks, or other security breaches. All users of cyberspace have some responsibility, not just for their own security, but also for the overall security and health of cyberspace.

In addition to the vulnerabilities in existing information technology systems, there are at least two other major barriers to users and managers acting to improve cybersecurity: (1) a lack of familiarity, knowledge, and

understanding of the issues; and (2) an inability to find sufficient numbers of adequately trained and/or appropriately certified personnel to create and manage secure systems.

Among the components of this priority are the following:

- Promote a comprehensive national awareness program to empower all Americans—businesses, the general workforce, and the general population— to secure their own parts of cyberspace;

- Foster adequate training and education programs to support the Nation's cybersecurity needs;

- Increase the efficiency of existing federal cybersecurity training programs; and

- Promote private sector support for well-coordinated, widely recognized professional cybersecurity certification.

Key to any successful national effort to enhance cybersecurity must be a national effort to raise awareness (of users and managers at all levels) and maintain an adequate pool of well trained and certified IT security specialists. The federal government cannot by itself create or manage all aspects of such an effort. It can only do so in partnership with industry, other governments, and nongovernmental actors.

Many federal agencies must play a part in this effort, which will be led and coordinated by DHS. The components of this program will include the following federal programs (both existing programs and initiatives which will be considered as part of the budget decision making process) and activities, which we recommend to our partners.

A. AWARENESS

1. **Promote a Comprehensive National Awareness Program to Empower All Americans—Businesses, the General Workforce, and the General Population—to Secure their Own Parts of Cyberspace**

In many cases solutions to cybersecurity issues exist, but the people who need them do not know they exist or do not know how or where to find them. In other cases people may not even be aware of the need to make a network element secure. A small business, for example, may not realize that the configuration of its web server uses a default password that allows anyone to gain control of the system. Education and outreach play an important role in making users and operators of cyberspace sensitive to security needs. These activities are an important part of the solution for almost all of the issues discussed in the *National Strategy to Secure*

Cyberspace, from securing digital control systems in industry, to securing broadband Internet access at home.

DHS, working in coordination with appropriate federal, state, and local entities and private sector organizations, will facilitate a comprehensive awareness campaign including audience-specific awareness materials, expansion of the StaySafeOnline campaign, and development of awards programs for those in industry making significant contributions to security. (A/R 3-1)

Increasing awareness and education prepares private sectors, organizations, and individuals to secure their parts of cyberspace. Actions taken by one entity on a network can immediately and substantially affect one or many others. Because the insecurity of one participant in cyberspace can have a major impact on the others, the actions they take to secure their own networks contribute to the security of the whole. For example, a few subverted servers recently enabled an attack on some of the Internet Domain Name System root servers and threatened to disrupt service for many users. Through improved awareness the Nation can stimulate actions to secure cyberspace by creating an understanding at all audience levels of both cybersecurity issues and solutions. DHS will lead an effort to increase cybersecurity awareness for key audiences:

a. Home Users and Small Business

Home users and small business are not part of the critical infrastructures. However, their systems are being increasingly subverted by malicious actors to attack critical systems. Therefore, increasing the awareness about cybersecurity among these users contributes to greater infrastructure security. Home users and small business owners of cyber systems often start with the greatest knowledge gap about cybersecurity.

DHS, in coordination with other agencies and private organizations, will work to educate the general public of home users, students, children, and small businesses on basic cyberspace safety and security issues. As part of these efforts, DHS will partner with the Department of Education and state and local governments to elevate the exposure of cybersecurity issues in primary and secondary schools. In addition, the Federal Trade Commission will continue to provide information on cybersecurity for consumers and small businesses through http://www.ftc.gov/infosecurity.

DHS, in coordination with the Department of Education, will encourage and support, where appropriate subject to budget considerations, state, local, and private organizations in the development of programs and guidelines for primary and secondary school students in cybersecurity. (A/R 3-2)

In recent years, with the spread of "always on" connections for systems, such as cable modems, digital subscriber lines (DSL), and wireless and satellite systems, the security of home user and small business systems has become more important not only to the users themselves, but to others to which they are connected through the Internet. For example, these connections generally mean that larger amounts of data can be sent and done so in a continuous stream. These two factors can be exploited and used to attack other systems, possibly even resulting in nationally significant damage. The Internet service providers, antivirus software companies, and operating system/application software developers that provide services or products to home users and small businesses can help raise their awareness of cybersecurity issues.

Home users and small businesses can help the Nation secure cyberspace by securing their own connections to it. Installing firewall software and updating it regularly, maintaining current antivirus software, and regularly updating operating systems and major applications with security enhancements are actions that individuals and enterprise operators can take to help secure cyberspace. To facilitate such actions, DHS will create a public-private task force of private

companies, organizations, and consumer users groups to identify ways that providers of information technology products and services, and other organizations can make it easier for home users and small businesses to secure their systems. (A/R 3-3)

b. Large Enterprises

The security of large enterprises is important not only to individual businesses, but to the Nation as a whole. Large enterprises own major cyber networks and computing systems that, if not secure, can be exploited for attacks on other businesses in an increasingly interconnected economy, and could, in the case of a massive attack, have major economic consequences. The cybersecurity of large enterprises can be improved through strong management to ensure that best practices and efficient technology are being employed, especially in the areas of configuration management, authentication, training, incident response, and network management. DHS will continue the work of sensitizing the owners of these networks to their vulnerabilities and what can be done to mitigate them. DHS, working with other government agencies and private sector organizations, will build upon and expand existing efforts to direct the attention of key corporate decision makers (e.g., CEOs and members of boards of directors) to the business case for securing their companies' information systems.

Decision makers can take a variety of steps to improve the security of their enterprise networks and to ensure that their networks cannot be maliciously exploited. *Large enterprises are encouraged to evaluate the security of their networks that impact the security of the Nation's critical infrastructures. Such evaluations might include: (1) conducting audits to ensure effectiveness and use of best practices; (2) developing continuity plans which consider offsite staff and equipment; and, (3) participating in industrywide information sharing and best practice dissemination. (A/R 3-4)*

(i) Insider Threats. Many cyber attacks on enterprise systems are perpetrated by trusted "insiders." Insiders are people trusted with legitimate access rights to enterprise information systems and networks. Such trusted individuals can pose a significant threat to the enterprise and beyond. The insider threat poses a key risk because it provides a potential avenue for individuals who seek to harm the Nation to gain access to systems that could support their malicious objectives. Effectively mitigating the insider threat requires policies, practices, and continued training. Three common policy areas which can reduce insider threat include: (1) access controls, (2) segregation of duties, and, (3) effective policy enforcement.

- Poor access controls enable an individual or group to inappropriately modify, destroy, or disclose sensitive data or computer programs for purposes such as personal gain or sabotage.

- Segregation of duties is important in assuring the integrity of an enterprise's information system. No one person should have complete control of any system.

- Effective enforcement of an enterprise security policy can be challenging and requires regular auditing. New automated software is beginning to emerge which can facilitate efficient enforcement of enterprise security. These programs allow the input of policy in human terms, translation to machine code, and then monitoring at the packet level of all data transactions within, and outbound from, the network. Such software can detect and stop inappropriate use of networks and cyber-based resources.

c. Institutions of Higher Education (IHEs)

Awareness plays an especially important role in increasing the cybersecurity of IHEs. As recent experience has shown, organized attackers have collectively exploited many insecure computer systems traceable to the campus networks of higher education as a platform from which to launch denial-of-service attacks and other threats to unrelated systems on the Internet. Such attacks harm not only the targeted systems, but also the owners of those systems and those who desire to use their services. IHEs are subject to exploitation for two reasons: (1) they possess vast amounts of computing power; and (2) they allow relatively open access to those resources. The computing power owned by IHEs is extensive, covering over 3,000 schools, many with research and significant central computing facilities.

The higher education community, collectively, has been actively engaged in efforts to organize its members and coordinate action to raise awareness and enhance cybersecurity on America's campuses. Most notably, through EDUCAUSE, the community has raised the issue of the Strategy's development with top leaders of higher education, including the American Council on Education and the Higher Education IT Alliance. Significantly, through this effort, top university presidents have adopted a 5-point Framework for Action that commits them to giving IT security high priority and to adopting the policies and measures necessary to realize greater system security:

(1) Make IT security a priority in higher education;

(2) Revise institutional security policy and improve the use of existing security tools;

(3) Improve security for future research and education networks;

(4) Improve collaboration between higher education, industry, and government; and

(5) Integrate work in higher education with the national effort to strengthen critical infrastructure.

Colleges and universities are encouraged to secure their cyber systems by establishing some or all of the following as appropriate: (1) one or more ISACs to deal with cyber attacks and vulnerabilities; (2) model guidelines empowering Chief Information Officers (CIOs) to address cybersecurity; (3) one or more sets of best practices for IT security; and, (4) model user awareness programs and materials. (A/R 3-5)

d. Private Sectors

DHS will work with private sectors on general awareness as well as on specific issues impacting particular sectors. Private sectors own and operate the vast majority of the Nation's cyberspace. As long time partners in the effort to secure cyberspace, many sectors have developed plans in parallel with the *National Strategy to Secure Cyberspace* to help secure their critical infrastructures. The sectors can serve a vital role in the reduction of vulnerabilities by creating sector-wide awareness of issues that affect multiple members. Members can develop and share best practices and work together toward common security solutions. For example, SCADA systems are a widespread security issue in the energy sector. Solutions are being coordinated with the Department of Energy and across the sector. The sectors also play a role in the identification of research needs. DHS will closely coordinate with private sectors on plans and initiatives to secure cyberspace.

A public-private partnership should continue work in helping to secure the Nation's cyber infrastructure through participation in, as appropriate and feasible, a technology and R&D gap analysis to provide input into the federal cybersecurity research agenda, coordination on the conduct of associated research, and the development and dissemination of best practices for cybersecurity. (A/R 3-6)

e. State and Local Governments

DHS will implement plans to focus key decision makers in state and local governments—such as governors, state legislatures, mayors, city managers, and county commissioners/boards of supervisors—to support investment in information systems security measures and adopt enforceable management policies and practices.

B. TRAINING

In addition to raising general awareness, the Nation must focus resources on training a talented and innovative pool of citizens that can specialize in securing the infrastructure. While the need for this pool has grown quickly with the expansion of the Internet and the pervasiveness of computers, networks, and other cyber devices, the investment in training has not kept pace. Universities are turning out fewer engineering graduates, and much of their resources are dedicated to other subjects, such as biology and life sciences. This trend must be reversed if the United States is to lead the world with its cyber economy.

1. Foster Adequate Training and Education Programs to Support the Nation's Cybersecurity Needs

Improvements in cybersecurity training will be accomplished primarily through the work of private training organizations, institutions of learning, and the Nation's school systems.

DHS will also encourage private efforts to ensure that adequate opportunities exist for continuing education and advanced training in the workplace to maintain high skills standards and the capacity to innovate.

The federal government can play a direct role in several ways. First, *DHS will implement and encourage the establishment of programs to advance the training of cybersecurity professionals in the United States, including coordination with NSF, OPM, and NSA, to identify ways to leverage the existing Cyber Corps Scholarship for Service program as well as the various graduate, postdoctoral, senior researcher, and faculty development fellowship and traineeship programs created by the*

Cyber Security Research and Development Act, to address these important training and education workforce issues. (A/R 3-7)

2. Increase the Efficiency of Existing Federal Cybersecurity Training Programs

Second, DHS will explore the benefits of a center for the development of cybersecurity training practices that would draw together expertise and be consistent with the federal "build once, use many" approach. *DHS, in coordination with other agencies with cybersecurity training expertise, will develop a coordination mechanism linking federal cybersecurity and computer forensics training programs. (A/R 3-8)*

C. CERTIFICATION

1. Promote Private Sector Support for Well-coordinated Widely Recognized Professional Cybersecurity Certifications

Related to education and training is the need for certification of qualified persons. Certification can provide employers and consumers with greater information about the capabilities of potential employees or security consultants. Currently, some certifications for cybersecurity workers exist; however, they vary greatly in the requirements they impose. For example, some programs emphasize broad knowledge verified by an extensive multiple-choice exam, while others verify in-depth

practical knowledge on a particular cyber component. No one certification offers a level of assurance about a person's practical and academic qualifications, similar to those offered by the medical and legal professions.

To address this issue, a number of industry stakeholders including representatives of both consumers and providers of IT security certifications are beginning to explore approaches to developing nationally recognized certifications and guidelines for certification.

Aspects that warrant consideration by these organizations include levels of education and experience, peer recognition, continuing education requirements, testing guidance, as applicable for various levels of certification that may be established, and models for administering a certification for IT security professionals similar to those successfully employed in other professions. DHS and other federal agencies, as downstream consumers (prospective employers of certified personnel), can aid these efforts by effectively articulating the needs of the federal IT security community.

DHS will encourage efforts that are needed to build foundations for the development of security certification programs that will be broadly accepted by the public and private sectors. DHS and other federal agencies can aid these efforts by effectively articulating the needs of the federal IT security community. (A/R 3-9)

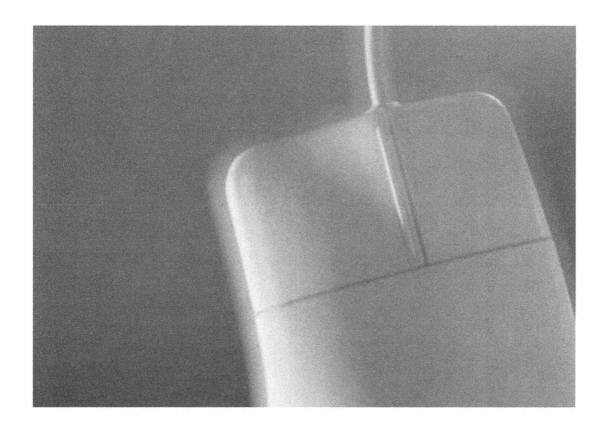

Priority IV: Securing Governments' Cyberspace

Although most critical infrastructures are in the private sector, governments at various levels perform many key functions. Among those key functions are national defense, homeland security, emergency response, taxation, payments to citizens, central bank activities, criminal justice, and public health. All of those functions and others now depend upon information networks and systems. Thus, it is the duty of governments to secure their information systems in order to provide essential services. At the federal level it is also required by law.

The foundation for the federal government's cybersecurity requires assigning clear and unambiguous authority and responsibility for security, holding officials accountable for fulfilling those responsibilities, and integrating security requirements into budget and capital planning processes.

The federal government will lead by example, giving cybersecurity appropriate attention and care, and encouraging others to do so. The federal government's procurement practices will be used to help promote cybersecurity. For example, federal agencies should become early adopters of new, more secure systems and protocols where appropriate.

State and local governments can have a similar effect on cybersecurity. The federal government is ready to partner with both state and local governments to promote cybersecurity.

Within the federal government the Director of OMB is responsible for ensuring that department and agency heads carry out their legal responsibilities to secure IT systems, with the exception of classified systems of national security departments and agencies that are the responsibility of the Secretary of Defense and the Director of Central Intelligence.

A. THE FEDERAL GOVERNMENT

Beginning with the Budget Blueprint in February 2001, continuing in the fiscal year 2002 and 2003 budgets, and the Management Reform Agenda, this administration has set a clear agenda for government reform. These reforms include unifying federal government security and critical infrastructure protection initiatives, and making strong security a condition of funding for all federal investments in information-technology systems.

The *National Strategy to Secure Cyberspace* supports these efforts by working to ensure that the federal government can identify vulnerabilities, anticipate threats, mitigate attacks when possible, and provide for continuity of operations.

To overcome deficiencies in cybersecurity, OMB established a governmentwide IT security program, as required by law, to set IT security policies and perform oversight of federal agency compliance with security requirements. This program is based on a cost-effective, risk-based approach. Agencies must ensure that security is integrated within every IT investment. This approach is designed to enable federal government business operations, not to unnecessarily impede those functions.

1. Continuously Assess Threats and Vulnerabilities to Federal Cyber Systems

A key step to ensuring the security of federal information technology is to understand the current state of the effectiveness of security and privacy controls in individual systems. Once identified, it is equally important to maintain that understanding through a continuing cycle of risk assessment. This approach is reflected in OMB security policies, and is featured in FISMA.

OMB's first report to Congress on government information security reform in February 2002 identified six common governmentwide security performance gaps.

These weaknesses included:

(1) Lack of senior management attention;

(2) Lack of performance measurement;

(3) Poor security education and awareness;

(4) Failure to fully fund and integrate security into capital planning and investment control;

(5) Failure to ensure that contractor services are adequately secure; and

(6) Failure to detect, report, and share information on vulnerabilities.

These gaps are not new or surprising. OMB, along with the General Accounting Office and agency inspectors general, has found them to be problems for at least 6 years. The evaluation and reporting requirements established by law have given OMB and federal agencies an opportunity to develop a comprehensive, cross-government baseline of agency IT security performance that had not been previously available. More importantly, through the development and use of corrective action plans, the federal government has a uniform process to track progress in fixing those weaknesses.

Before OMB approves funding for a system an agency must demonstrate that it has resolved outstanding security issues related to the system. Additionally, agencies must ensure that security has been incorporated and security costs reported for every IT investment through the federal capital planning process. OMB policy stipulates that specific lifecycle security costs be identified, built into, and funded as part of each system investment. Failure to do so results in disapproval of funding for the entire system.

2. Agency-Specific Processes

The federal government must have a comprehensive and crosscutting approach to improving cybersecurity. Three processes central to improving and maintaining federal cybersecurity in the agencies are: identifying and documenting enterprise architectures; continuously assessing threats and vulnerabilities, and understanding the risks they pose to agency operations and assets; and implementing security controls and remediation efforts to reduce and manage those risks. Each agency will be expected to create and implement this formal three-step process to achieve greater security.

a. Identify and Document Enterprise Architectures

OMB policy requires each agency to identify and document their enterprise architecture, including an authoritative inventory of all operations and assets, all agency IT systems, critical business processes, and their interrelationships with other organizations. This process yields a governmentwide view of critical security needs.

Through the budget process, the federal government will drive agency investments in commercially available tools to improve their architectures and system configuration. Configuration management and control has incidental and important benefits to security. For example, controlling system configuration

permits agencies to more effectively and efficiently enforce policies and permissions and more easily install antivirus definitions and other software updates and patches across an entire system or network.

b. Continuously Assess Threats and Vulnerabilities

Commercially available automated auditing and reporting mechanisms should be used to validate the effectiveness of the security controls across a system and are essential to continuously understand risks to those systems. These tools can help in analyzing data, providing forward-looking assessments, and alerting agencies of unacceptable risks to their operations.

Federal agencies will continue to expand the use of automated, enterprise-wide security assessment and security policy enforcement tools and actively deploy threat management tools to deter attacks. The federal government will determine whether specific actions are necessary (e.g., through the policy or budget processes) to promote the greater use of these tools. (A/R 4-1)

c. Implement Security Controls and Remediation Efforts

The implementation of security controls that maintain risk at an acceptable level can often be accomplished in a relatively brief amount of time. However, the remediation of vulnerabilities is a much more complex challenge. Software is constantly changing and each new upgrade can introduce new vulnerabilities. As a result, vulnerabilities must be assessed continuously. Remediation often involves "patching" or installing pieces of software or code that are used to update the main program. The remediation of federal systems must be planned in a consistent fashion.

B. ADDITIONAL GOVERNMENTWIDE CHALLENGES

In addition, there are four specific government-wide security challenges that need to be addressed. Each agency, as appropriate, should work with OMB to resolve these challenges.

1. Authenticate and Maintain Authorization for Users of Federal Systems

Identifying and authenticating each system user is the first link in the system security chain, and it must take place whenever system access is initiated. To establish and maintain secure system operations, organizations must ensure that the people on the system are who they say they are and are doing only what they are authorized to do. Many authentication procedures used today are inadequate. Passwords are not being changed from the system default, are often incorrectly configured, and are rarely updated.

The federal government will continue to promote a continuing chain of security for all federal employees and processes, including the use, where appropriate, of biometric smart cards for access to buildings and computers, and authentication from the moment of computer log on. The benefits of such an approach are clear. By promoting multi-layered identification and authentication—the use of strong passwords, smart tokens, and biometrics - the federal government will eliminate many significant security problems that it has today.

Through the ongoing E-Authentication initiative, the federal government will review the need for stronger access control and authentication; explore the extent to which all departments can employ the same physical and logical access control tools and authentication mechanisms; and consequently, further promote consistency and interoperability. (A/R 4-2)

The National Information Assurance Partnership (NIAP)

NIAP is a U.S. Government initiative to meet testing, evaluation, and assessment needs of both information technology (IT) producers and consumers. NIAP is a collaboration between the National Institute of Standards and Technology (NIST) and the National Security Agency (NSA) in fulfilling their respective responsibilities under the Computer Security Act of 1987.

The partnership, originated in 1997, combines the extensive security experience of both agencies to promote the development of technically sound security requirements for IT products and systems and appropriate metrics for evaluating those products and systems. The long-term goal of NIAP is to help increase the level of trust consumers have in their information systems and networks through the use of cost-effective security testing, evaluation, and assessment programs. NIAP continues to build important relationships with government agencies and industry in a variety of areas to help meet current and future IT security challenges affecting the Nation's critical information infrastructure. More information on the partnership can be found at http://www.niap.nist.gov.

2. Secure Federal Wireless Local Area Networks

When using wireless technology, the federal government will carefully evaluate the risks associated with using such technology for critical functions. The National Institute of Standards and Technology (NIST) notes that wireless communications can be intercepted and that wireless networks can also experience denial-of-service attacks. Federal agencies should use the NIST findings and recommendations on wireless systems as a guide to the operation of wireless networks.

Federal agencies should consider installing systems that continuously check for unauthorized connections to their networks. Agency policy and procedures should reflect careful consideration of additional risk reduction measures, including the use of strong encryption, bi-directional authentication, shielding standards and other technical security considerations, configuration management, intrusion detection, incident handling, and computer security awareness and training programs. (A/R 4-3)

3. Improve Security in Government Outsourcing and Procurement

Through a joint effort of OMB's Office of Federal Procurement Policy, the Federal Acquisition Regulations Council, and the Executive Branch Information Systems Security Committee, the federal government is identifying ways to improve security in agency contracts and evaluating the overall federal procurement process as it relates to security. Agencies' maintenance of security for outsourced operations was cited as one of the key weaknesses identified in OMB's February 2002 security report to Congress.

Additionally, the federal government will be conducting a comprehensive review of the National Information Assurance Partnership (NIAP), to determine the extent to which it is adequately addressing the continuing problem of security flaws in commercial software products. This review will include lessons learned from implementation of the Defense Department's July 2002 policy requiring the acquisition of products reviewed under the NIAP or similar evaluation processes. (A/R 4-4)

Department of Defense (DOD) policy stipulates that if an evaluated product of the type being sought is available for use, then the DOD component must procure the evaluated product. If no evaluated product is currently available, the component must require prospective

vendors to submit their product for evaluation to be further considered.

Following this program review, the government will evaluate the cost effectiveness of expanding the program to cover all federal agencies. If this proves workable, it could both improve government security and leverage the government's significant purchasing power to influence the market and begin to improve the security of all consumer information technology products.

4. Develop Specific Criteria for Independent Security Reviews and Reviewers and Certification

With the growing emphasis on security comes the corresponding need for expert independent verification and validation of agency security programs and practices. FISMA and OMB's implementing guidance require that agencies' program officials and CIOs review at least annually the status of their programs. Few agencies have available personnel resources to conduct such reviews, and thus they frequently contract for such services. Agencies and OMB have found that contractor security expertise varies widely from the truly expert to less than acceptable. Moreover, many independent verification and validation contractors are also in the business of providing security program implementation services; thus, their program reviews may be biased toward their preferred way of implementing security.

The federal government will explore whether private sector security service providers to the federal government should be certified as meeting certain minimum capabilities, including the extent to which they are adequately independent. (A/R 4-5)

C. STATE AND LOCAL GOVERNMENTS

American democracy is rooted in the precepts of federalism—a system of government in which power is allocated between federal and state governments. This structure of overlapping federal, state, and local governance has more than 87,000 different jurisdictions and provides unique opportunity and challenges for cyberspace security efforts. State and local governments, like the federal government, operate large, interconnected information systems upon which critical government services depend.

States provide services that make up the "public safety net" for millions of Americans and their families. Services include essential social support activities as well as critical public safety functions, such as law enforcement and emergency response services. States also own and operate critical infrastructure systems, such as electric power and transmission, transportation, and water systems. They play a catalytic role in bringing together the different stakeholders that deliver critical services within their state to prepare for, respond to, manage, and recover from a crisis. Delivering critical services unique to their roles and responsibilities within our federalist system makes state government a critical infrastructure sector in its own right.

Many of these critical functions carried out by states are inexorably tied to IT—including making payments to welfare recipients, supporting law enforcement with electronic access to criminal records, and operating state-owned utility and transportation services. Preventing cyber attacks and responding quickly when they do occur, ensures that these 24/7 systems remain available and in place to provide important services that the public needs and expects. Information technology systems

have the potential for bringing unprecedented efficiency and responsiveness from state governments for their residents. Citizen confidence in the integrity of these systems and the data collected and maintained by them is essential for expanded use and capture of these potential benefits.

With an increasing dependence on integrated systems, state, local, and federal agencies have to collectively combat cyber attacks. Sharing information to protect systems is an important foundation for ensuring government continuity. States have adopted several mechanisms to facilitate the sharing of information on cyber attacks and in reporting incidents.

These mechanisms are continually modified and improved as new policy emerges and as technological solutions become available. In addition, states are exploring options for improving information sharing both internally and externally. These options include enacting legislation that provides additional funding and training for cybersecurity and forming partnerships across state, local, and federal governments to manage cyber threats.

1. DHS will Work with State and Local Governments and Encourage them to Consider Establishing IT Security Programs and to Participate in ISACs with Similar Governments

State and local governments are encouraged to establish IT security programs for their departments and agencies, including awareness, audits, and standards; and to participate in the established ISACs with similar governments. (A/R 4-6)

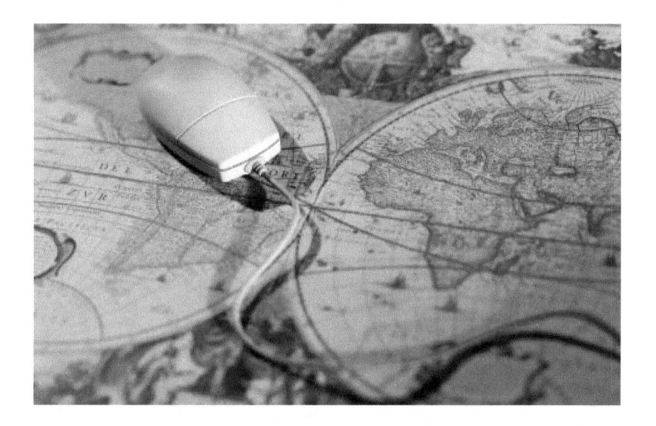

Priority V: National Security and International Cyberspace Security Cooperation

America's cyberspace is linked to that of the rest of the world. Attacks cross borders at light speed. Distinguishing between malicious activity originating from criminals, nation state actors, and terrorists in real time is difficult. This requires America to be prepared to defend critical networks and respond to attacks in each case. Systems supporting this country's critical national defense and the intelligence community must be secure, reliable, and resilient—able to withstand attack regardless of the origin of attack. America must also be prepared to respond as appropriate to attacks against its critical infrastructure. At the same

time, America must be ready to lead global efforts, working with governments and industry alike, to secure cyberspace that is vital to the operation of the world's economy and markets. Global efforts require raising awareness, promoting stronger security standards, and aggressively investigating and prosecuting cybercrime.

A. ENSURING AMERICA'S NATIONAL SECURITY

We face adversaries, including nation states and terrorists, who could launch cyber attacks or seek to exploit our systems. In peacetime America's enemies will conduct espionage against our government, university research centers, and private companies. Activities would likely include mapping U.S. information systems, identifying key targets, lacing our infrastructure with "back doors" and other means of access. In wartime or crisis, adversaries may seek to intimidate by attacking critical infrastructures and key economic functions or eroding public confidence in information systems. They may also attempt to slow the U.S. military response by disrupting systems of the Department of Defense (DoD), the Intelligence Community, and other government organizations as well as critical infrastructures.

America has already experienced significant national cybersecurity events. In 1998, attackers carried out a sophisticated, tightly orchestrated series of cyber intrusions into the computers of DoD, NASA, and government research labs. The intrusions were targeted against those organizations that conduct advanced technical research on national security, including atmospheric and oceanographic topics as well as aircraft and cockpit design.

The United States must have the capability to secure and defend systems and infrastructures that are deemed national security assets, and develop the capability to quickly identify the origin of malicious activity. We must improve our national security posture in cyberspace to limit the ability of adversaries to conduct espionage or pressure the United States.

1. Strengthen Counterintelligence Efforts in Cyberspace

The FBI and intelligence community should ensure a strong counterintelligence posture to counter cyber-based intelligence collection against the United States government, and commercial and educational organizations. This effort must include a deeper understanding of the capability and intent of our adversaries to use cyberspace as a means for espionage. (A/R 5-1)

2. Improve Attack Attribution and Prevention Capabilities

The intelligence community, DoD, and the law enforcement agencies must improve the Nation's ability to quickly attribute the source of threatening attacks or actions to enable timely and effective response. Consistent with the National Security Strategy, these efforts will also seek to develop capabilities to prevent attacks from reaching critical systems and infrastructures. (A/R 5-2)

3. Improve Coordination for Responding to Cyber Attacks within the United States National Security Community

The United States must improve interagency coordination between law enforcement, national security, and defense agencies involving cyber-based attacks and espionage, ensuring that criminal matters are referred, as appropriate, among those agencies. The National Security Council and the Office of Homeland Security will lead a study to ensure that appropriate mechanisms are in place. (A/R 5-3)

4. Reserve the Right to Respond in an Appropriate Manner

When a nation, terrorist group, or other adversary attacks the United States through cyberspace, the U.S. response need not be limited to criminal prosecution. The United States reserves the right to respond in an appropriate manner. The United States will be prepared for such contingencies. (A/R 5-4)

B. INTERNATIONAL COOPERATION

The Department of State will lead federal efforts to enhance international cyberspace security cooperation. Key initiatives include:

1. Work through International Organizations and with Industry to Facilitate and to Promote a Global "Culture of Security"

America's interest in promoting global cybersecurity extends beyond our borders. Our information infrastructure is directly linked with Canada, Mexico, Europe, Asia, and South America. The United States and world economy increasingly depend upon global markets and multinational corporations connected via information networks. The vast majority of cyber attacks originates or passes through systems abroad, crosses several borders, and requires international investigative cooperation to be stopped.

Global networks supporting critical economic and security operations must be secure and reliable. Securing global cyberspace will require international cooperation to raise awareness, increase information sharing, promote security standards, and investigate and prosecute those who engage in cybercrime. The United States is committed to working with nations to ensure the integrity of the global information networks that support critical economic and security infrastructure. We are also ready to utilize government-sponsored organizations such as the Organization of Economic Cooperation and Development (OECD), G-8, the Asia Pacific Economic Cooperation forum (APEC), and the Organization of American States (OAS), and other relevant organizations to facilitate global coordination on cybersecurity. In order to facilitate coordination with the private sector, we will also utilize such organizations as the Transatlantic Business Dialogue.

2. Develop Secure Networks

The United States will engage in cooperative efforts to solve technical, scientific, and policy-related problems to assure the integrity of information networks. We will encourage the development and adoption of international technical standards and facilitate collaboration and research among the world's best scientists and researchers. We will promote such efforts as the OECD's *Guidelines for the Security of Information Systems and Networks*, which strive to inculcate a "culture of security" across all participants in the new information society.

Because most nations' key information infrastructures reside in private hands, the United States will seek the participation of United States industry to engage foreign counterparts in a peer-to-peer dialogue, with the twin objectives of making an effective business case for cybersecurity, and explaining successful means for partnering with government on cybersecurity.

The United States will work through appropriate international organizations and in partnership with industry to facilitate dialogue between foreign public and private sectors on information infrastructure protection and promote a global "culture of security." (A/R 5-5)

3. Promote North American Cyberspace Security

The United States will work with Canada and Mexico to make North America a "Safe Cyber Zone." We will expand programs to identify and secure critical common networks that underpin telecommunications, energy, transportation, banking and finance systems, emergency services, food, public health, and water systems. (A/R 5-6)

4. Foster the Establishment of National and International Watch-and-Warning Networks to Detect and Prevent Cyber Attacks as they Emerge

The United States will urge each nation to build on the common Y2K experience and appoint a centralized point-of-contact who can act as a liaison between domestic and global cybersecurity efforts. Establishing points of contact can greatly enhance the international coordination and resolution of cyberspace security issues. We will also encourage each nation to develop its own watch-and-warning network capable of informing government agencies, the public, and other countries about impending attacks or viruses. (A/R 5-7)

To facilitate real-time sharing of the threat information as it comes to light, the United States will foster the establishment of an international network capable of receiving, assessing, and disseminating this information globally. Such a network can build on the capabilities of nongovernmental institutions such as the Forum of Incident Response and Security Teams. (A/R 5-8)

The United States will encourage regional organizations, such as the APEC, EU, and OAS, to each form or designate a committee responsible for cybersecurity. Such committees would also benefit from establishing parallel working groups with representatives from the private sector. The United States will also encourage regional organizations—such as the APEC, EU, and OAS—to establish a joint committee on cybersecurity with representatives from government and the private sector. (A/R 5-9)

5. Encourage Other Nations to Accede to the Council of Europe Convention on Cybercrime, or to Ensure that their Laws and Procedures are at Least as Comprehensive

The United States will actively foster international cooperation in investigating and prosecuting cybercrime. The United States has signed and supports the recently concluded Council of Europe Convention on Cybercrime, which requires countries to make cyber attacks a substantive criminal offense and to adopt procedural and mutual assistance measures to better combat cybercrime across international borders.

The United States will encourage other nations to accede to the Council of Europe Convention on Cybercrime or to ensure that their laws and procedures are at least as comprehensive. (A/R 5-10)

Ongoing multilateral efforts, such as those in the G-8, APEC, and OECD are also important. The United States will work to implement agreed-upon recommendations and action plans that are developed in these forums. Among these initiatives, the United States in particular will urge countries to join the 24-hour, high-tech crime contact network begun within the G-8, and now expanded to the Council of Europe membership, as well as other countries.

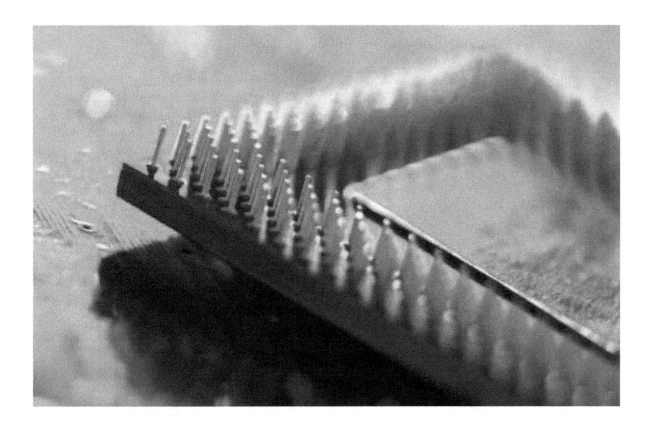

Conclusion: The Way Forward

Our reliance on cyberspace will only continue to grow in the years ahead. Cyberspace and the networks that connect to it now support our economy and provide for our national and homeland defense. This national dependency must be managed with continuous efforts to secure the cyber systems that control our infrastructures.

Securing cyberspace is a complex and evolving challenge. *The National Strategy to Secure Cyberspace* was developed in close collaboration with key sectors of the economy that rely on cyberspace, state and local governments, colleges and universities, and concerned organizations. Town hall meetings were held around the country, and fifty-three clusters of key questions were published to spark public debate.

In addition, a draft version of the *National Strategy to Secure Cyberspace* was shared with the Nation for public comment. The response has been overwhelming.

The public-private partnerships that formed in response to the President's call have developed their own strategies to protect the parts of cyberspace on which they rely. This unique partnership and process was and will continue to be necessary because the majority of the country's cyber resources are controlled by entities outside of government. For the *National Strategy to Secure Cyberspace* to work it must be a plan in which a broad cross section of the country is both invested and committed. Accordingly, the dialogue about how we secure cyberspace will continue.

The *National Strategy to Secure Cyberspace* identifies five national priorities that will help us achieve this ambitious goal. These are: (1) a national cyberspace security response system; (2) a national cyberspace security threat and vulnerability reduction program; (3) a national cyberspace security awareness and training program; (4) securing governments' cyberspace; and, (5) national security and international cyberspace security cooperation. These five priorities will serve to prevent, deter, and protect against attacks. In addition, they also create a process for minimizing the damage and recovering from attacks that do occur.

The *National Strategy to Secure Cyberspace* is, however, only a first step in a long-term effort to secure our information infrastructures. The federal executive branch will use a variety of tools to implement this *Strategy.* The Administration will work with Congress to craft future federal security budgets based on the *Strategy,* providing every department and agency involved in cybersecurity with resources to execute its responsibilities. Each lead department and agency will plan and program to execute the initiatives assigned by the *National Strategy to Secure Cyberspace.*

Within the federal government DHS will play a central role in implementing the *National Strategy to Secure Cyberspace.* In addition to executing its assigned initiatives, the Department would also serve as the primary federal point-of-contact for state and local governments, the private sector, and the American people on issues related to cyberspace security. Working with the White House, the Department therefore would coordinate and support implementation of non-federal tasks recommended in the *National Strategy to Secure Cyberspace.*

Each department and agency will also be accountable for its performance on cyberse-curity efforts. The federal government will employ performance measures—and encourage the same for state and local governments—to evaluate the effectiveness of the cybersecurity programs outlined in this *Strategy.* These performance measures will allow agencies to measure their progress, make resource allocation decisions, and adjust priorities accordingly.

Federal, state, and local governments, as well as organizations and people all across the United States will continue to work to improve cyberspace security. As these strategies and plans are implemented, we will begin to incrementally reduce threats and vulnerabilities.

Cybersecurity and personal privacy need not be opposing goals. Cyberspace security programs must strengthen, not weaken, such protections. The federal government will continue to regularly meet with privacy advocates to discuss cybersecurity and the implementation of this *Strategy.*

For the foreseeable future, two things will be true: America will rely upon cyberspace and the federal government will seek a continuing broad partnership to develop, implement, and refine the *National Strategy to Secure Cyberspace.*

Actions and Recommendations (A/R) Summary

Priority I: A National Cyberspace Security Response System

A/R 1-1: DHS will create a single point-of-contact for the federal government's interaction with industry and other partners for 24 x7 functions, including cyberspace analysis, warning, information sharing, major incident response, and national-level recovery efforts. Private sector organizations, which have major contributions for those functions, are encouraged to coordinate activities, as permitted by law, in order to provide a synoptic view of the health of cyberspace on a 24 x 7 basis.

A/R 1-2: As outlined in the 2003 budget, the federal government will complete the installation of CWIN to key government cybersecurity-related network operation centers, to disseminate analysis and warning information and perform crisis coordination. The federal government will also explore linking the ISACs to CWIN.

A/R 1-3: To test civilian agencies' security preparedness and contingency planning, DHS will use exercises to evaluate the impact of cyber attacks on governmentwide processes. Weaknesses discovered will be included in agency corrective action plans and submitted to the OMB. DHS also will explore such exercises as a way to test the coordination of public and private incident management, response and recovery capabilities.

A/R 1-4: Corporations are encouraged to regularly review and exercise IT continuity plans and to consider diversity in IT service providers as a way of mitigating risk.

A/R 1-5: Infrastructure sectors are encouraged to establish mutual assistance programs for cybersecurity emergencies. DoJ and the Federal Trade Commission should work with the sectors to address barriers to such cooperation, as appropriate. In addition, DHS's Information Analysis and Infrastructure Protection Directorate will coordinate the development and regular update of voluntary joint government-industry cybersecurity contingency plans, including a plan for recovering Internet functions.

A/R 1-6: DHS will raise awareness about the removal of impediments to information sharing about cybersecurity and infrastructure vulnerabilities between the public and private sectors. The Department will also establish an infrastructure protection program office to manage the information flow, including the development of protocols for how to care for "voluntarily submitted critical infrastructure information."

A/R 1-7: Corporations are encouraged to consider active involvement in industrywide programs to share information on IT security, including the potential benefits of joining an appropriate ISAC. Colleges and universities are encouraged to consider establishing: (1) one or more ISACs to deal with cyber attacks and vulnerabilities; and, (2) an on-call point-of-contact to Internet service providers and law enforcement officials in the event that the school's IT systems are discovered to be launching cyber attacks.

Priority II: A National Cyberspace Security Threat and Vulnerability Reduction Program

A/R 2-1: DoJ and other appropriate agencies will develop and implement efforts to reduce cyber attacks and cyber threats through the following means: (1) identifying ways to improve information sharing and investigative coordination within the federal, state, and local law enforcement community working on critical infrastructure and cyberspace security matters, and with other agencies and the private sector; (2) exploring means to provide sufficient investigative and forensic resources and training to facilitate expeditious investigation and resolution of critical infrastructure incidents; and, (3) developing better data about victims of cybercrime and intrusions in order to understand the scope of the problem and be able to track changes over time.

A/R 2-2: DHS, in coordination with appropriate agencies and the private sector, will lead in the development and conduct of a national threat assessment including red teaming, blue teaming, and other methods to identify the impact of possible attacks on a variety of targets.

A/R 2-3: The Department of Commerce will form a task force to examine the issues related to IPv6, including the appropriate role of government, international interoperability, security in transition, and costs and benefits. The task force will solicit input from potentially impacted industry segments.

A/R 2-4: DHS, in coordination with the Commerce Department and appropriate agencies, will coordinate public-private partnerships to encourage: (1) the adoption of improved security protocols; (2) the development of more secure router technology; and, (3) the adoption by ISPs of a "code of good conduct," including cybersecurity practices and security related cooperation. DHS will support

these efforts as required for their success, subject to other budget considerations.

A/R 2-5: DHS, in coordination with DOE and other concerned agencies and in partnership with industry, will develop best practices and new technology to increase security of DCS/SCADA, to determine the most critical DCS/SCADA-related sites, and to develop a prioritized plan for short-term cybersecurity improvements in those sites.

A/R 2-6: DHS will work with the National Infrastructure Advisory Council and private sector organizations to develop an optimal approach and mechanism for vulnerability disclosure.

A/R 2-7: GSA will work with DHS on an improved approach to implementing a patch clearinghouse for the federal government. DHS will also share lessons learned with the private sector and encourage the development of a voluntary, industry-led, national effort to develop a similar clearinghouse for other sectors including large enterprises.

A/R 2-8: The software industry is encouraged to consider promoting more secure "out-of-the-box" installation and implementation of their products, including increasing: (1) user awareness of the security features in products; (2) ease-of-use for security functions; and, (3) where feasible, promotion of industry guidelines and best practices that support such efforts.

A/R 2-9: DHS will establish and lead a public-private partnership to identify cross-sectoral interdependencies both cyber and physical. The partnership will develop plans to reduce related vulnerabilities in conjunction with programs proposed in the National Strategy for Homeland Security. The National Infrastructure Simulation and Analysis Center in DHS will support these efforts by developing models to identify the impact of cyber and physical interdependencies.

A/R 2-10: DHS also will support, when requested and as appropriate, voluntary efforts by owners and operators of information system networks and network data centers to develop remediation and contingency plans to reduce the consequences of large-scale physical damage to facilities supporting such networks, and to develop appropriate procedures for limiting access to critical facilities.

A/R 2-11: To meet these needs, the Director of OSTP will coordinate the development, and update on an annual basis a federal government research and development agenda that includes near-term (1-3 years), mid-term (3-5 years), and later (5 years out and longer) IT security research for Fiscal Year 2004 and beyond. Existing priorities include, among others, intrusion detection, Internet infrastructure security (including protocols such as BGP and DNS), application security, DoS, communications security (including SCADA system encryption and authentication), high-assurance systems, and secure system composition.

A/R 2-12: To optimize research efforts relative to those of the private sector, DHS will ensure that adequate mechanisms exist for coordination of research and development among academia, industry and government, and will develop new mechanisms where needed.

A/R 2-13: The private sector is encouraged to consider including in near-term research and development priorities, programs for highly secure and trustworthy operating systems. If such systems are developed and successfully evaluated, the federal government will, subject to budget considerations, accelerate procurement of such systems.

A/R 2-14: DHS will facilitate a national public-private effort to promulgate best practices and methodologies that promote integrity, security, and reliability in software code development, including processes and procedures that diminish the possibilities of erroneous code, malicious code, or trap doors that could be introduced during development.

A/R 2-15: DHS, in coordination with OSTP and other agencies, as appropriate, will facilitate communication between the public and private research and the security communities, to ensure that emerging technologies are periodically reviewed by the appropriate body within the National Science and Technology Council, in the context of possible homeland and cyberspace security implications, and relevance to the federal research agenda.

Priority III: A National Cyberspace Security Awareness and Training Program

A/R 3-1: DHS, working in coordination with appropriate federal, state, and local entities and private sector organizations, will facilitate a comprehensive awareness campaign including audience-specific awareness materials, expansion of the StaySafeOnline campaign, and development of awards programs for those in industry making significant contributions to security.

A/R 3-2: DHS, in coordination with the Department of Education, will encourage and support, where appropriate subject to budget considerations, state, local, and private organizations in the development of programs and guidelines for primary and secondary school students in cybersecurity.

A/R 3-3: Home users and small businesses can help the Nation secure cyberspace by securing their own connections to it. Installing firewall software and updating it regularly, maintaining current antivirus software, and regularly updating operating systems and major applications with security enhancements are actions that individuals and enterprise operators can take to help secure cyberspace. To facilitate such actions, DHS will create a public-private task force of private companies, organizations, and consumer users groups to identify ways that providers of information technology products and services, and other organizations can make it easier for home users and small businesses to secure their systems.

A/R 3-4: Large enterprises are encouraged to evaluate the security of their networks that impact the security of the Nation's critical infrastructures. Such evaluations might include: (1) conducting audits to ensure effectiveness and use of best practices; (2) developing continuity plans which consider offsite staff and equipment; and, (3) participating in industrywide information sharing and best practices dissemination.

A/R 3-5: Colleges and universities are encouraged to secure their cyber systems by establishing some or all of the following as appropriate: (1) one or more ISACs to deal with cyber attacks and vulnerabilities; (2) model guidelines empowering Chief Information Officers (CIOs) to address cybersecurity; (3) one or more sets of best practices for IT security; and, (4) model user awareness programs and materials.

A/R 3-6: A public-private partnership should continue work in helping to secure the Nation's cyber infrastructure through participation in, as appropriate and feasible, a technology and R&D gap analysis to provide input into the federal cybersecurity research agenda, coordination on the conduct of associated research, and the development and dissemination of best practices for cybersecurity.

A/R 3-7: DHS will implement and encourage the establishment of programs to advance the training of cybersecurity professionals in the United States, including coordination with NSF, OPM, and NSA, to identify ways to leverage the existing Cyber Corps Scholarship for Service program as well as the various graduate, postdoctoral, senior researcher, and faculty development fellowship and traineeship programs created by the Cyber Security Research and Development Act, to address

these important training and education workforce issues.

A/R 3-8: DHS, in coordination with other agencies with cybersecurity training expertise, will develop a coordination mechanism linking federal cybersecurity and computer forensics training programs.

A/R 3-9: DHS will encourage efforts that are needed to build foundations for the development of security certification programs that will be broadly accepted by the public and private sectors. DHS and other federal agencies can aid these efforts by effectively articulating the needs of the Federal IT security community.

Priority IV: Securing Governments' Cyberspace

A/R 4-1: Federal agencies will continue to expand the use of automated, enterprise-wide security assessment and security policy enforcement tools and actively deploy threat management tools to deter attacks. The federal government will determine whether specific actions are necessary (e.g., through the policy or budget processes) to promote the greater use of these tools.

A/R 4-2: Through the ongoing E-Authentication initiative, the federal government will review the need for stronger access control and authentication; explore the extent to which all departments can employ the same physical and logical access control tools and authentication mechanisms; and, consequently, further promote consistency and interoperability.

A/R 4-3: Federal agencies should consider installing systems that continuously check for unauthorized connections to their networks. Agency policy and procedures should reflect careful consideration of additional risk reduction measures, including the use of strong encryption, bi-directional authentication, shielding standards and other technical security considerations, configuration management, intrusion detection, incident handling, and computer security awareness and training programs.

A/R 4-4: Additionally, the federal government will be conducting a comprehensive review of the National Information Assurance Partnership (NIAP), to determine the extent to which it is adequately addressing the continuing problem of security flaws in commercial software products. This review will include lessons-learned from implementation of the Defense Department's July 2002 policy requiring the acquisition of products reviewed under the NIAP or similar evaluation processes.

A/R 4-5: The federal government will explore whether private sector security service providers to the federal government should be certified as meeting certain minimum capabilities, including the extent to which they are adequately independent.

A/R 4-6: State and local governments are encouraged to establish IT security programs for their departments and agencies, including awareness, audits, and standards; and to partic- ipate in the established ISACs with similar governments.

Priority V: National Security and International Cyberspace Security Cooperation

A/R 5-1: The FBI and intelligence community should ensure a strong counterintelligence posture to counter cyber-based intelligence collection against the U.S. Government, and commercial and educational organizations. This effort must include a deeper understanding of the capability and intent of our adversaries to use cyberspace as a means for espionage.

A/R 5-2: The intelligence community, DoD, and the law enforcement agencies must improve the Nation's ability to quickly attribute the source of threatening attacks or actions to

enable timely and effective response. Consistent with the *National Security Strategy*, these efforts will also seek to develop capabil- ities to prevent attacks from reaching critical systems and infrastructures.

A/R 5-3: The United States must improve interagency coordination between law enforcement, national security, and defense agencies involving cyber-based attacks and espionage, ensuring that criminal matters are referred, as appropriate, among those agencies. The National Security Council and the Office of Homeland Security will lead a study to ensure that appropriate mechanisms are in place.

A/R 5-4: When a nation, terrorist group, or other adversary attacks the United States through cyberspace, the U.S. response need not be limited to criminal prosecution. The United States reserves the right to respond in an appro- priate manner. The United States will be prepared for such contingencies.

A/R 5-5: The United States will work through appropriate international organizations and in partnership with industry to facilitate dialogue between foreign public and private sectors on information infrastructure protection and promote a global "culture of security."

A/R 5-6: The United States will work with Canada and Mexico to make North America a "Safe Cyber Zone." We will expand programs to identify and secure critical common networks that underpin telecommunications, energy, transportation, banking and finance systems, emergency services, food, public health, and water systems.

A/R 5-7: The United States will urge each nation to build on the common Y2K experience and appoint a centralized point-of-contact who can act as a liaison between domestic and global cybersecurity efforts. Establishing points of contact can greatly enhance the international coordination and resolution of cyberspace security issues. We will also encourage each nation to develop its own watch-and-warning network capable of informing government agencies, the public, and other countries about impending attacks or viruses.

A/R 5-8: To facilitate real-time sharing of the threat information as it comes to light; the United States will foster the establishment of an international network capable of receiving, assessing, and disseminating this information globally. Such a network can build on the capabilities of nongovernmental institutions such as the Forum of Incident Response and Security Teams.

A/R 5-9: The United States will encourage regional organizations, such as the APEC,

EU, and OAS, to each form or designate a committee responsible for cybersecurity. Such committees would also benefit from establishing parallel working groups with representatives from the private sector. The United States will also encourage regional organizations—such as the APEC, EU, and OAS—to establish a joint committee on cybersecurity with representatives from government and the private sector.

A/R 5-10: The United States will encourage other nations to accede to the Council of Europe Convention on Cybercrime or to ensure that their laws and procedures are at least as comprehensive.

CPSIA information can be obtained
at www.ICGtesting.com
Printed in the USA
LVHW100313250519
619118LV00027B/234/P